OLD TESTAMENT MESSAGE

A Biblical-Theological Commentary

Carroll Stuhlmueller, C.P. and Martin McNamara, M.S.C.
EDITORS

Old Testament Message, Volume 16

ESTHER, JUDITH, TOBIT, JONAH, RUTH

John Craghan, C.SS.R.

Michael Glazier, Inc.
Wilmington, Delaware

First published in 1982 by:
MICHAEL GLAZIER, INC.
1723 Delaware Avenue
Wilmington, Delaware 19806

Distributed outside U.S., Canada & the Philippines by:
GILL & MACMILLAN, LTD.
Goldenbridge, Inchicore
Dublin 8 Ireland

©1982 by Michael Glazier, Inc.
All rights reserved.

Library of Congress Catalog Card Number: 81-85270
International Standard Book Number
  Old Testament Message series: 0-89453-235-9
  ESTHER, JUDITH, TOBIT, JONAH, RUTH
  0-89453-249-9 (Michael Glazier, Inc.)
  7171-1179-2 (Gill and Macmillan Ltd.)

The Bible text in this publication is from the Revised Standard Version of the
Bible, copyrighted 1946, 1952, ©1971, 1973 by the Division of Christian Education
of the National Council of the Churches of Christ in the U.S.A., and used by
permission.

Cover design by Lillian Brulc

Printed in the United States of America

TABLE OF CONTENTS

IN
GRATEFUL MEMORY
OF
MY FATHER
JOHN F. CRAGHAN, SR.
(1896-1978)

Editors' Preface

Old Testament Message brings into our life and religion today the ancient word of God to Israel. This word, according to the book of the prophet Isaiah, had soaked the earth like "rain and snow coming gently down from heaven" and had returned to God fruitfully in all forms of human life (Isa 55:10). The authors of this series remain true to this ancient Israelite heritage and draw us into the home, the temple and the market place of God's chosen people. Although they rely upon the tools of modern scholarship to uncover the distant places and culture of the biblical world, yet they also refocus these insights in a language clear and understandable for any interested reader today. They enable us, even if this be our first acquaintance with the Old Testament, to become sister and brother, or at least good neighbor, to our religious ancestors. In this way we begin to hear God's word ever more forcefully in our own times and across our world, within our prayer and worship, in our secular needs and perplexing problems.

Because life is complex and our world includes, at times in a single large city, vastly different styles of living, we have much to learn from the Israelite Scriptures. The Old Testament spans forty-six biblical books and almost nineteen hundred years of life. It extends through desert, agricultural and urban ways of human existence. The literary style embraces a world of literature and human emotions. Its history began with Moses and the birth-pangs of a new people, it came of age politically and economically under David and Solomon, it reeled under the fiery threats of prophets like Amos and Jeremiah. The people despaired and yet were re-created with new hope during the Babylonian exile. Later reconstruction in the homeland and then the trauma of apocalyptic movements prepared for the revelation of "the mystery hidden for ages in God who created all things" (Eph 3:9).

While the Old Testament telescopes twelve to nineteen hundred years of human existence within the small country of Israel, any single moment of time today witnesses to the reenactment of this entire history across the wide expanse of planet earth. Each verse of the Old Testament is being relived somewhere in our world today. We need, therefore, the *entire* Old Testament and all twenty-three volumes of this new set, in order to be totally a "Bible person" within today's widely diverse society.

The subtitle of this series—"A Biblical-Theological Commentary"—clarifies what these twenty-three volumes intend to do.

Their *purpose* is theological: to feel the pulse of God's word for its *religious* impact and direction.

Their *method* is biblical: to establish the scriptural word firmly within the life and culture of ancient Israel.

Their *style* is commentary: not to explain verse by verse but to follow a presentation of the message that is easily understandable to any serious reader, even if this person is untrained in ancient history and biblical languages.

Old Testament Message—like its predecessor, *New Testament Message*—is aimed at the entire English-speaking world and so is a collaborative effort of an international team. The twenty-one contributors are women and men drawn from North America, Ireland, Britain and Australia. They are scholars who have published in scientific journals, but they have been chosen equally as well for their proven ability to communicate on a popular level. This twenty-three book set comes from Roman Catholic writers, yet, like the Bible itself, it reaches beyond interpretations restricted to an individual church and so enables men and women rooted in biblical faith to unite and so to appreciate their own traditions more fully and more adequately.

Most of all, through the word of God, we seek the blessedness and joy of those

who walk in the law of the Lord!...

who seek God with their whole heart (Ps. 119:1-2).

CARROLL STUHLMUELLER, C.P.   MARTIN McNAMARA, M.S.C.

GENERAL INTRODUCTION

The five biblical books treated in this volume are stories, i.e., narratives which seek to arouse tension and then resolve it. However, they are more than ancient stories of God and humans. They are our stories as well. They challenge us to uncover the basic human experiences of life and death, success and failure, hope and despair. They urge us to gain new perspectives and regain lost values.

The basic challenge reflected in these books is community-identity-liberty. We are tempted to find our identity solely within ourselves and to see liberty as being free *from* others. These books, however, force us to seek our identity only within the context of community and to understand liberty as being free *for* others. We cannot be dropouts from society. Rather, we must interact with our sisters and brothers to rediscover the proper notion of freedom.

In proposing models for such human liberation, these biblical books offer more heroines than heroes. Esther, Judith, Naomi, and Ruth demonstrate the delicate art of coping and caring but in a remarkably feminine way. Despite their male-dominated society they are able to break free in order to pursue the common good. They are examples, not only of women's liberation, but also of truly human liberation. They are persons for others.

The Book of Esther

CONTENTS

INTRODUCTION TO
THE BOOK OF ESTHER

The Appeal of the Book

People can make a difference. People do make a difference. The author of the Hebrew text of Esther did not believe in a divine monopoly. Humans were not so many puppets to be pulled at the right moment for the execution of the divine plan. People — and here God's people — had to take their rightful place in history and make their contribution to the common good. The author believed that to abdicate from the social scene, to turn the control of the world over to God, and to be dropouts from history was not only self-defeating but also dehumanizing. The Hebrew text of Esther is a vote of confidence in human effort.

From rags to riches. The hero of the account, Mordecai, is an exile from the land of Israel. The heroine of the story, Esther, is an orphan. God's own people are powerless Diaspora Jews. However, the end of the story presents a different picture. Mordecai is the prime minister, second only to the powerful king of Persia. Esther is the queen of Persia, enjoying perhaps more influence over the king than Mordecai. Finally the Jews are first-rate citizens who have earned the respect and fear of fellow Persians.

Reversal is a key device for telling the story. Esther is not unlike the Joseph story of Genesis. An apparently insignificant Hebrew can overcome all odds and attain his moment in the sun. It is as second to Pharaoh that Joseph prospers in a foreign land and benefits both Egyptians and Hebrews. The author of Esther had learned well from the rags to riches story of biblical Joseph.

The story of Esther and Mordecai lives on, not only in the Bible but also in the Jewish celebration of Purim. (In the Hebrew Bible Esther is found in the third division, i.e., the Writings, as one of the five festal scrolls, viz., for the feast of Purim.) In this carnival-like celebration with its costumes and disguises joy is the element which pervades. Indeed the Talmud permits the free consumption of wine to the point where the distinction between "Blessed be Mordecai" and "Cursed be Haman" becomes blurred. However, it is the text which teaches the Jew how to celebrate. The celebration of Purim in chap. 9 is in tension with the banqueting in chap. 1 and chaps. 5-6. To cope with one's moment in history, whether in ancient Persia or elsewhere, is always a more than adequate reason to celebrate. Purim, like the Book of Esther, is concerned not merely with surviving but with living.

The Setting of the Book

The story begins during the third year of the reign of King Ahasuerus, i.e., Xerxes I (486-465 B.C.). It is the splendor and pageantry of the Persian Empire (539-332 B.C.) which provides the setting for the Book of Esther. The author develops the plot, not in the hinterland of the great empire, but in the capital city of Susa. His characters will play their parts at court with all the intrigue associated with royal harems and scheming politicians. Indeed it will be the rejection of one queen (Vashti) which will occasion another's (Esther) rise. Again it will be the professional competition for high office that will implicate the Jews in the fate of Mordecai. Without the court setting the story would lose much of its luster. It would also be less effective in teaching the Jewish audience how to cope.

The story opens with an exotic description of the opulence and glamour of the Persian king and his entourage in Susa. Only in chap. 2 does the author mention Mordecai as an insignificant inhabitant of the same city. At the end of the story, however, King Ahasuerus is flanked by Prime Minister Mordecai. To account for this success, the author narrates the insubordination of Mordecai vis-à-vis the then prime minister, Haman. The insubordination then becomes an attack on the entire Jewish population in the empire. To offset the proposed annihilation, Mordecai intercedes with Esther who then intercedes with Ahasuerus.

It is at this point that Esther becomes the principal character in the story (see 4:17). Her schemes result in Haman's downfall, Mordecai's climb up the political ladder, and the thwarting of Haman's execution of the Jews. In chap. 9 the Jewish victory in Susa and the provinces provides the setting for the celebration of the feast of Purim. We somehow feel that Esther's name should appear alongside Mordecai's in the concluding verses.

Origins and Literary Form

The author of the Hebrew text has provided a compact story which reads well. Most likely the story or similar ones were circulating in Diaspora Jewry. It is difficult to isolate the different elements in the story, although some authors see the story as the merging of different traditions by a gifted writer. At best we can only suggest some of the traditions without attempting to explain how they eventually came together.

The most obvious element seems to be the feast of Purim in chap. 9. In the commentary we will discuss its rather complex history. For the moment it will be sufficient to note that it does not have the lion's share of the text. Although some authors would hold that the Book of Esther is a festal legend, i.e., a fictitious account to explain the feast, the disproportionate number of verses in the rest of the story would seem to argue against such a view.

Another element is the sage at a foreign court. The competition between Mordecai and Haman has certain parallels, not only with the Joseph story mentioned above, but also with Dan 2-6. In these tales the principals are endangered, usually because of a conspiracy linked with religion. They then face condemnation to death or imprisonment. Finally, however, they are released and recognition of their wisdom gives way to their exaltation. There are differences, however, since in Daniel it is God's intervention which effects the release and exoneration of the heroes.

Because of the presence of wisdom some would suggest that Esther is an historicized wisdom tale. It thus seeks to inculcate in story form the virtues and qualities expressed, e.g., in Proverbs and Qoheleth. However, the link with the feast of Purim would argue against such a suggestion. While the story does contain wisdom elements, the author does not accentuate wisdom *per se*.

Another element is a persecution of the Jews in the Persian Empire. Although there is no historical proof of the events narrated in Esther, it is not unlikely that there were pogroms in the Persian Empire directed against the Jewish population. However, because of exaggerations (see the banqueting and beauty pageant in chaps. 1-2) and anachronisms (Mordecai would be over a hundred years old according to 2:6) Esther is not history. Though many of the details fit Persian history and customs, the author's intent is not to write history.

Perhaps the best description of the literary form of Esther is "historical novel." Admittedly we cannot control the historical dimension. But it is clear that our author intends both to entertain and to teach. Thus, the story is more history-like than history. At the same time our willingness to trust the author, to let him tell the story according to his canons is a more rewarding approach. Our question, therefore, is not: was Esther really queen of Persia? It is, rather: what will the author tell us by making Esther queen of Persia?

The Author's Purpose

The Hebrew text of the Book of Esther does not mention the name of the God of Israel once. This is surprising when contrasted with the mention of the king of Persia 190 times in 167 verses. To be sure, the author does not deny the influence of God in human affairs. However, it is a hidden causality, viz., a causality where God chooses to trust his creatures in the formidable task of running a peculiarly human world.

The author implies that Jews are not to be reluctant to assume their responsibility in the world of Diaspora. He emphasizes the fact that they do count and they can make a difference. The world of the Persians is not something to be avoided at all costs but an arena which challenges them to contribute to both the state and their own people and thus their God. Significantly, while the author uses the term "Jew(s)," he never employs "Israel."

The author thus endorses a dual allegiance, i.e., allegiance to the Persian government and allegiance to the Jewish people. Both Esther and Mordecai are persons who seek the good of the crown. At the same time they are Jews who pursue the good of their fellow Jews. The author shrewdly intimates that Jews who support both the crown and their own people eventually overcome the difficulties which dual allegiance may seem to involve. The fate of the individual is necessarily bound up with the fate of both the nation and the Jewish people.

The author appears to nuance this dual allegiance. The ongoing existence of Israel depends on the conscious effort of Jews to support their fellow Jews, even when such efforts call for drastic actions. A tension thereby exists between the good of Israel and the good of the foreign government. By consciously choosing to opt for the good of Israel, the Jew paradoxically opts for the good of Persia. By overcoming Haman's plot against the Jews, Esther and Mordecai thus provide for the good of the Persian Empire.

Although there is mention of fasting, the traditional elements of Judaism are missing. When the Jewish population learns of the decree of annihilation, they don sackcloth and ashes but do not pray. When the Jews gather to celebrate the deliverance from the enemies, they exchange gifts and make merry but they do not thank the Lord. On the other hand, the Jewish identity of Esther eventually becomes a ploy in offsetting Haman's plans of extermination. We might conclude that we have overt Jews but covert Judaism. However, our author subtly argues that to meet the needs of fellow Jews (and thus the common good of the empire) is to remain faithful to the God of the covenant. To be a good Jew (and thus a good Persian) entails more than invoking the name of Yahweh.

The challenge of the Book of Esther is ongoing. It provokes Christians to note the needs of the state and yet not compromise their Christianity. It directs Christians to act responsibly in government: to serve the Christian good is to serve the common good. The book does not endorse masquerading in pious words and adopting pious language. It suggests confronting the problems of society with the understanding that the individual finds identity in the community. It also challenges the modern-day counterparts of Esther and Mordecai to react to the total biblical message, hence the New Testament. While the concrete way of reacting to today's needs will necessarily differ, the willingness to contribute remains the same.

Time of Composition

The many references to Persian life and government, the abundance of Persian loanwords, and the absence of Greek loanwords seem to call for a date sometime in the Persian period, perhaps in the fourth or fifth century B.C. Moreover, the Hebrew of the book suits such a period rather than the second century B.C. The book is certainly a product of the eastern Diaspora.

The above applies to the Hebrew text of the Book of

Esther. The Greek text, which exists in two divergent forms, is later and adds some 107 verses to the Hebrew text. These are the six so-called deuterocanonical additions to the Hebrew text which may be original Greek compositions rather than translations from a Hebrew original. They are significant because they are solutions to problems found in the Hebrew text. For example, the third or "C" addition attributes prayers to both Esther and Mordecai. The second and fifth additions ("B" and "E") cite documents and thus purport to lend historical testimony to the story. Although these additions are deuterocanonical and a good example of ongoing dialogue with the Hebrew text, limitations of space preclude their use in this commentary.

THE ELEVATION OF ESTHER
1:1-2:23.

The first two chapters narrate the steps which eventually lead to Esther's queenship. The final scene also suggests Mordecai's future elevation. The material may be divided as follows: (1) the banquets of Ahasuerus and Vashti (1:1-9); (2) the deposing of Vashti and the search for a new queen (1:10-22); (3) the beauty contest (2:1-14); (4) Esther, the beauty queen (2:15-18); (5) Esther, Mordecai and the plot against the king (2:19-23).

THE BANQUETS OF AHASUERUS AND VASHTI
1:1-9.

1 In the days of Ahasuerus, the Ahasuerus who reigned from India to Ethiopia over one hundred and twenty-seven provinces, ²in those days when King Ahasuerus sat on his royal throne in Susa the capital, ³in the third year of his reign he gave a banquet for all his princes and servants, the army chiefs of Persia and Media and the nobles and governors of the provinces being before him, ⁴while he showed the riches of his royal glory and the splendor and pomp of his majesty for many days, a hundred and eighty days. ⁵And when these days were completed, the king gave for all the people present in

Susa the capital, both great and small, a banquet lasting for seven days, in the court of the garden of the king's palace. ⁶There were white cotton curtains and blue hangings caught up with cords of fine linen and purple to silver rings and marble pillars, and also couches of gold and silver on a mosaic pavement of porphyry, marble, mother-of-pearl and precious stones. ⁷Drinks were served in golden goblets, goblets of different kinds, and the royal wine was lavished according to the bounty of the king. ⁸And drinking was according to the law, no one was compelled; for the king had given orders to all the officials of his palace to do as every man desired. ⁹Queen Vashti also gave a banquet for the women in the palace which belonged to King Ahasuerus.

The opening scene introduces the reader to the pomp and pageantry of the Persian court. Ahasuerus is the quintessence of power and pleasure. Yet the king who rules 127 provinces (but see Dan 6:3; 9:1) will not rule Vashti or Esther. In his acropolis (rather than "capital") at Susa he demonstrates his lavishness by hosting two banquets: (1) one lasting six months for the officials of the empire (see Jdt 1:16); (2) another lasting seven days for all the people in Susa. The author also elaborates on the ornate furnishings of the Persian court, employing many foreign and unique words to create an exotic impression (see Isa 3:18-23; Cant 4:13-14). Although Persian women were not secluded from banquets, Vashti hosts a third banquet for the women. Perhaps v.9 merely suggests that Vashti will not be manipulated by Ahasuerus.

Royal power or kingship is a recurring motif in Esther. This opening scene abounds with such statements as "royal throne" (v.2), "reign" (v.3), "royal glory" (v.4), "king's palace" (v.5) (better: "pavilion"), "royal wine" (v.7), etc. Ironically the non-regulation of drinking is even according to royal decree. (Verse 8 should be translated: "and the drinking was according to the royal decree of no compulsion.") Yet, while the drinking admits no compulsion and is within the law, Vashti will exhibit lack of compulsion and so be against the law. This motif of royal power is linked with the rise of both Esther and Mordecai to positions of influence. One wonders how a Jewish orphan and an insignificant Jewish exile can possibly match the king who rules 127 provinces.

The banquet is another prominent motif in the book. The book opens with Ahasuerus' two banquets. The book concludes with two banquets or celebrations, viz., Purim which is held on the 14th of Adar in the provinces and on the 15th in Susa (9:17-18). In the middle of the book Esther hosts two banquets for Ahasuerus and Haman (5:4-5, 8). The significance of the banquets is the disempowering of influential people. The banquets will be the setting for the fall of Vashti and Haman. In turn, the same setting will lead to the rise of Esther, Mordecai, and the Jewish people. The banquets are more than a delightful scene to capture the pomp of the court.

THE DEPOSING OF VASHTI AND
THE SEARCH FOR A NEW QUEEN
1:10-22.

[10]On the seventh day, when the heart of the king was merry with wine, he commanded Mehuman, Biztha, Harbona, Bigtha and Abagtha, Zethar and Carkas, the seven eunuchs who served King Ahasuerus as chamberlains, [11]to bring Queen Vashti before the king with her royal crown, in order to show the peoples and the princes her beauty; for she was fair to behold. [12]But Queen Vashti refused to come at the king's command conveyed by the eunuchs. At this the king was enraged, and his anger burned within him.

[13]Then the king said to the wise men who knew the times — for this was the king's procedure toward all who were versed in law and judgment, [14]the men next to him being Carshena, Shethar, Admatha, Tarshish, Meres, Marsena, and Memucan, the seven princes of Persia and Media, who saw the king's face, and sat first in the

kingdom—: [15]"According to the law, what is to be done to Queen Vashti, because she has not performed the command of King Ahasuerus conveyed by the eunuchs?" [16]Then Memucan said in presence of the king and the princes, "Not only to the king has Queen Vashti done wrong, but also to all the princes and all the peoples who are in all the provinces of King Ahasuerus. [17]For this deed of the queen will be made known to all women, causing them to look with contempt upon their husbands, since they will say, 'King Ahasuerus commanded Queen Vashti to be brought before him, and she did not come.' [18]This very day the ladies of Persia and Media who have heard of the queen's behavior will be telling it to all the king's princes, and there will be contempt and wrath in plenty. [19]If it please the king, let a royal order go forth from him, and let it be written among the laws of the Persians and the Medes so that it may not be altered, that Vashti is to come no more before King Ahasuerus; and let the king give her royal position to another who is better than she. [20]So when the decree made by the king is proclaimed throughout all his kingdom, vast as it is, all women will give honor to their husbands, high and low." [21]This advice pleased the king and the princes, and the king did as Memucan proposed; [22]he sent letters to all the royal provinces, to every province in its own script and to every people in its own language, that every man be lord in his own house and speak according to the language of his people.

The author underlines the male chauvinism of the Persians. While in his cups after a long bout of banqueting, Ahasuerus wishes to display his queen as a sex object (presumably she is to appear in full royal attire). The name "Vashti" sounds like the Hebrew word for "drinking" in v.8 and thus suggests that the action of the king is related to his condition. The author also infers the inferior condition of the women by noting in 1:9 that the place where the women assemble belongs to the king. The author is actually provoking a sense of humor among his readership by implying that the Persians do not know how to treat women. Indeed the king's advisers (v.13: "who knew the times," i.e., who know the laws and the proper legal procedure to follow), specifically Memucan, must conclude that Vashti's action will serve as a precedent and hence all women will look down on their husbands. Indeed the women will rebel (v.18 — rather than " 'will be telling' ") against the king's princes. To resolve their plight, the Persian men must resort to a royal decree. To add to the humor, Vashti's name does not even appear in the royal document which is dispatched by the elaborate communications system of the Persians.

This scene also introduces another motif of the book, viz., obedience/disobedience. It is the disobedience of Vashti which provides the occasion for Esther's entrance to court. Ironically, whereas Vashti's disobedience provokes the king's wrath, Esther's disobedience (5:2) will incite the king's mercy. Ahasuerus thus deposes one inflexible queen only to acquire a more inflexible one.

Linked with the motif of obedience/disobedience is the irrevocability of the laws of the Persians and the Medes (see Dan 6:8, 9, 12, 15). Although there is no historical proof for this (it also militates against good legislation), our author introduces the notion to anticipate the decrees of Haman (3:11-15) and Mordecai (8:8-14). The question arises: how can one offset the whole chain of events that Haman has set in motion by the irrevocable decree?

THE BEAUTY CONTEST
2:1-14.

2 After these things, when the anger of King Ahasuerus had abated, he remembered Vashti and what she had done and what had been decreed against her. ²Then the king's servants who attended him said, "Let beautiful young virgins be sought out for the king. ³And let the king appoint officers in all the provinces of his kingdom to gather all the beautiful young virgins to the harem in Susa the capital, under custody of Hegai the king's eunuch who is in charge of the women; let their ointments be given them. 4And let the maiden who pleases the king be queen instead of Vashti." This pleased the king, and he did so.

5Now there was a Jew in Susa the capital whose name was Mordecai, the son of Jair, son of Shimei, son of Kish, a Benjaminite, 6who had been carried away from Jerusalem among the captives carried away with Jeconiah king of Judah, whom Nebuchadnezzar king of Babylon had carried away. 7He had brought up Hadassah, that is Esther, the daughter of his uncle, for she had neither father nor mother; the maiden was beautiful and lovely, and when her father and her mother died, Mordecai adopted her as his own daughter. 8So when the king's order and his edict were proclaimed, and when many maidens were gathered in Susa the capital in custody of Hegai, Esther also was taken into the king's palace and put in custody of Hegai who had charge of the women. 9And the maiden pleased him and won his favor; and he quickly provided her with her ointments and her portion of food, and with seven chosen maids from the king's palace, and advanced her and her maids to the best place in the harem. 10Esther had not made known her people or kindred, for Mordecai had charged her not to make it known. 11And every day Mordecai walked in front of the court of the harem, to learn how Esther was and how she fared.

12Now when the turn came for each maiden to go in to King Ahasuerus, after being twelve months under the regulations for the women, since this was the regular period of their beautifying, six months with oil of myrrh and six months with spices and ointments for women— 13when the maiden went in to the king in this way she was given whatever she desired to take with her from the harem to the king's palace. 14In the evening she went, and in the morning she came back to the second harem in custody of Shaashgaz the king's eunuch who was in charge of the concubines; she did not go in to the king again, unless the king delighted in her and she was summoned by name.

The search for a new queen begins. Besides being beautiful and a virgin, the new queen should also be obedient to the king, unlike the recalcitrant Vashti. In the search the pleasures of the king are paramount. According to 2:16 (see 1:3) the process of testing virgins takes four years. However, the king's sexual delights also call for a twelve-month beauty treatment: six months with oil of myrrh and another six months with balsam and other cosmetics. The beauty process smacks of the exotic/erotic. In Cant 4:3, for example, the Beloved wears a pouch of myrrh and the Lover rests between her breasts (see also Ps 45 [44]:9-10; Prov 7:17). At the same time the text distinguishes between Vashti/Esther and the other maidens. Only the two queens are beautiful (1:11; 2:7) while all the other maidens are merely good to look at (v.2 should be translated thus rather than " 'beautiful' ").

The author now introduces Mordecai. His name resembles that of the Babylonian god Marduk. The name *Marduka* appears in the early fifth century B.C. as the name of an accountant who was part of an inspection tour from Susa. In introducing Mordecai, the author indicates that he does not intend to write sober history. He makes Mordecai an exile of the deportation of King Jehoiachin in 597 B.C. (see 2 Kgs 24:6-17). He would have been at least 122 years old upon becoming prime minister in the twelfth year of Ahasuerus (3:7). Presumably Esther would have been 100 years his junior.

The author offers a very imposing family tree for Mordecai and thus prepares the reader for his dispute with Haman. Shimei is the Benjaminite who cursed David (see 2 Sam 16:5) and Kish is the father of Israel's first king, Saul (see 1 Sam 9:1-2). He thus belongs to a family which has an implacable enmity with the Amalekites who will be represented by Haman. Significantly the author does not provide a Davidic genealogy for Mordecai. The Saulide origin suits the atmosphere of the Diaspora where a Davidic restoration (see Haggai, Zechariah, Chronicler) was impossible. In the

Book of Esther Israel will defeat her enemies in the absence of an autonomous monarch.

The author also introduces Esther for the first time. Her name sounds like that of the Babylonian goddess of love, Ishtar. However, it may come from a Persian word meaning "star." Like Daniel (see Dan 1:6-7), she has a Jewish name as well, Hadassah, which according to the Aramaic translations means "myrtle." In this initial scene Esther is not only a beautiful virgin but also the obedient foster daughter of Mordecai. She takes no initiative since Mordecai makes all the decisions for her, such as telling her to conceal her Jewish ancestry. He also checks up on her everyday, as he solicits information about her progress.

The author is preparing the reader for the moment when Esther will make the decisions and Mordecai will take orders. (Unlike Ahasuerus, Mordecai is ruler of his household.) In v.9 the Hebrew verb suggests that Esther actively provoked the favor of Hegai. This results in her starting the beauty process immediately and enjoying the expertise of special attendants. The portions of food contrast with the scene in 4:16 where Esther and her maids will fast. It also anticipates the feast of Purim in 9:19, 22 where the celebration entails food gifts (to give portions is to have power). The special favor Esther has won from Hegai looks forward to the king's favorable reaction (2:18).

ESTHER, THE BEAUTY QUEEN
2:15-18.

> 15When the turn came for Esther the daughter of Abihail the uncle of Mordecai, who had adopted her as his own daughter, to go in to the king, she asked for nothing except what Hegai the king's eunuch, who had charge of the women, advised. Now Esther found favor in the eyes of all who saw her. 16And when Esther was taken to King Ahasuerus into his royal palace in the tenth month, which is the month of Tebeth, in the seventh year of his reign, 17the king loved Esther more than all the women, and she

found grace and favor in his sight more than all the virgins, so that he set the royal crown on her head and made her queen instead of Vashti. [18] Then the king gave a great banquet to all his princes and servants; it was Esther's banquet. He also granted a remission of taxes to the provinces, and gave gifts with royal liberality.

In approaching the king, Esther follows the sage advice of Hegai. Whereas v.13 allows the maiden to take whatever she wants, Esther chooses to rely on the eunuch's knowledge of the king's preferences. The reader is not surprised at the outcome since Esther has already gained the favor of all the spectators. Vashti's refusal anticipated Esther's success. Whereas Vashti had declined to wear the royal crown at the banquet (1:12), Esther complies.

The king's choice necessarily leads to a banquet, since feasting and power go together. The scene is thus tied in with the feast of Purim. In celebrating their new power, the Jews will act like King Ahasuerus. They will give gifts and they will rest (9:17, 22). "Rest" is from the same root as the phrase "remission of taxes." The RSV also notes that it may be translated "holiday." Esther's accession is symbolic of the Jewish accession.

ESTHER, MORDECAI, AND THE PLOT AGAINST THE KING
2:19-23.

[19]When the virgins were gathered together the second time, Mordecai was sitting at the king's gate. [20]Now Esther had not made known her kindred or her people, as Mordecai had charged her; for Esther obeyed Mordecai just as when she was brought up by him. [21]And in those days, as Mordecai was sitting at the king's gate, Bigthan and Teresh, two of the king's eunuchs, who guarded the threshold, became angry and sought to lay hands on King Ahasuerus. [22]And this came to the knowledge of Mordecai, and he told it to Queen Esther, and Esther told the

king in the name of Mordecai. [23]When the affair was investigated and found to be so, the men were both hanged on the gallows. And it was recorded in the Book of Chronicles in the presence of the king.

This concluding section of chap. 2 seems to be a doublet of 2:8-10. The expression "the second time" should probably be rendered "to resume," hence a repetition of the gathering of the maidens and Esther's obedience to Mordecai. However, the repetition is quite likely the deliberate intention of the author. Thus, Esther's obedience is underlined to contrast with 4:17 where Mordecai will obey Esther's commands. It further suggests the moment when Esther will disobey the king's law (5:1-5). It also raises the question whether Esther will comply with Mordecai's request to intercede with the king in 4:8-17.

The motif of obedience/disobedience is pursued in vv.21-23. Mordecai seems to occupy some position at court ("sitting at the king's gate" — see Dan 2:49). Owing to such circumstances he perhaps learns of a plot to assassinate the king. His loyalty to the king is thus beyond question. Yet the following verses will speak of Haman's promotion, not Mordecai's, and of Mordecai's disobedience in failing to do obeisance to Haman. It seems almost a contradiction that prime minister Haman will promote a decree against the Jews after such a demonstration on Mordecai's part of loyalty to the crown. One almost wonders if Mordecai's duly recorded loyalty will somehow come to the king's attention. The author is obviously preparing the reader for the king's insomnia and the catalyst which brings about Mordecai's promotion and Haman's demise (6:1-3).

HAMAN'S PLOT
TO DESTROY THE JEWS
3:1-4:17.

These two chapters narrate the situation which leads to the decree and finally to Mordecai's request for Esther's help. The material may be divided as follows: (1) Mordecai's insubordination and Haman's reprisals (3:1-7); (2) the decree against the Jews (3:8-15); (3) Mordecai's request of Esther's aid (4:1-17).

MORDECAI'S INSUBORDINATION AND
HAMAN'S REPRISALS
3:1-7.

3 After these things King Ahasuerus promoted Haman the Agagite, the son of Hammedatha, and advanced him and set his seat above all the princes who were with him. ²And all the king's servants who were at the king's gate bowed down and did obeisance to Haman; for the king had so commanded concerning him. But Mordecai did not bow down or do obeisance. ³Then the king's servants who were at the king's gate said to Mordecai, "Why do you transgress the king's command?" ⁴And when they spoke to him day after day and he would not listen to them, they told Haman, in order to see whether Mordecai's words would avail; for he had told them that he was a Jew. [5]And when Haman saw that Mordecai did not bow down or do obeisance to him, Haman was filled with fury. [6]But he disdained to lay hands on Mordecai alone. So, as they had made known to him the people of Mordecai, Haman sought to destroy all the Jews, the people of Mordecai, throughout the whole kingdom of Ahasuerus. [7]In the first month, which is the month of Nisan, in the twelfth year of King Ahasuerus, they cast Pur, that is the lot, before Haman day after day; and they cast it month after month till the twelfth month, which is the month of Adar.

The chapter opens with a statement of Haman's promotion to prime minister ("set his seat above all the princes"). Given Mordecai's proof of loyalty to the crown in chap. 2, one naturally expects him to be somewhat disgruntled at Haman's good fortune. While the fierce competition between the two rivals offers some explanation of Mordecai's insubordination, the basic reason is more nationalistic. The statement of Mordecai's Jewish origins in v.4 is set against the prime minister's family tree, i.e., he is an Agagite. The Amalekites, a desert people, were Israel's traditional enemies from time of the Exodus (see Exod 17:8-16; Deut 25:17-19). In 1 Sam 15:1-9 King Saul routs Agag, king of the Amalekites, and his troops. However, Saul spares Agag while his troops unlawfully plunder the camp of the enemy, an action which provokes Samuel's wrath and Saul's subsequent dismissal as king (see 1 Sam 15:10-31).

In the Book of Esther the nationalistic antagonism between Haman/Amalekites and Mordecai/Saulides explains Haman's desire to annihilate the Jewish people because of Mordecai's effrontery. True to his family roots, Mordecai imitates his ancestor Shimei (2:5) who refused obeisance to King David when the king was forced to flee (see 2 Sam 16:5-14). The Saulide associations also elucidate the Jewish action in 9:10, 15-16 where the Jews do not plunder despite 8:11. By refusing to plunder, the Jews honor the obligation which Saul and his troops disregarded. Once again the motif of kingship emerges.

The motif of obedience/disobedience arises as well. Haman's desire to avenge Mordecai's insubordination is itself an act of disobedience since he decides on the plan (v.6) prior to seeking the approval of the king. (As the story develops, his plans miscarry.)

THE DECREE AGAINST THE JEWS
3:8-15.

[8]Then Haman said to King Ahasuerus, "There is a certain people scattered abroad and dispersed among the peoples in all the provinces of your kingdom; their laws are different from those of every other people, and they do not keep the king's laws, so that it is not for the king's profit to tolerate them. [9]If it please the king, let it be decreed that they be destroyed, and I will pay ten thousand talents of silver into the hands of those who have charge of the king's business, that they may put it into the king's treasuries." [10]So the king took his signet ring from his hand and gave it to Haman the Agagite, the son of Hammedatha, the enemy of the Jews. [11]And the king said to Haman, "The money is given to you, the people also, to do with them as it seems good to you."

[12]Then the king's secretaries were summoned on the thirteenth day of the first month, and an edict, according to all that Haman commanded, was written to the king's satraps and to the governors over all the provinces and to the princes of all the peoples, to every province in its own script and every people in its own language; it was written in the name of King Ahasuerus and sealed with the king's ring. [13]Letters were sent by couriers to all the king's provinces, to destroy, to slay, and to annihilate all Jews, young and old, women and children, in one day, the thirteenth day of the twelfth month, which is the month of Adar, and to plunder their goods. [14]A copy of the document was to be issued as a decree in every province by proclamation to all the peoples to be ready for that day.

[15]The couriers went in haste by order of the king, and the decree was issued in Susa the capital. And the king

and Haman sat down to drink; but the city of Susa was perplexed.

To win the king's approval, Haman accuses the Jews of having different laws — a custom sanctioned, however, by the Persians. Although Mordecai had not kept the law, still Haman's accusation that the Jews do not keep the laws is a false generalization. Haman then promises to add 10,000 talents to the state coffers. The amount offered is considerable. One author estimated it some six years ago to be equivalent to $18,000,000 before inflation began.

What is Haman's intended action against the Jews? The verb in v.9, "to be destroyed," may also be translated "cause to become homeless." This suggests that Haman wants the king to think in terms of slavery. It is such slavery that will add the 10,000 talents to the royal treasury. The reader knows from v.6 that Haman wishes to destroy the Jews. However, in keeping with his deceitful character he suggests slavery while he is really proposing annihilation. Although such an explanation is not without difficulties, it explains to some degree the king's reaction to Esther's request in 8:5-8, viz., the effort to avert the intended slaughter.

Haman's wish becomes an imperial decree and is duly promulgated with the efficient machinery of the Persian bureaucracy. Mordecai's disobedience has set in motion the annihilation of his people in the empire. The reader wonders if somehow the crisis can be averted and the power struggle between Haman and Mordecai resolved more amicably. The rest of the book seeks to show how the disobedient Mordecai can rise in the ranks and how the disobedient Esther can offset the apparent catastrophe to her people.

Feasting/banqueting is also in evidence. Verse 7 introduces the word *pur*, i.e., "lot," which will eventually become the name of the Jewish feast of Purim. (Verse 7 probably means that they cast the lot once to determine the day and the month of the slaughter.) According to v.12 the fate of the Jews was determined the day before they were to celebrate Passover. The feast marking Israel's liberation is thus in the shadow of the event marking Israel's annihilation in the empire. Finally, in v.15, while the city of Susa is thrown into confusion, Ahasuerus and Haman sit down to drink, i.e., to celebrate the forthcoming destruction of the supposedly disobedient people. As the story develops, it will be in the setting of another banquet that Esther will undo the reason for this celebration.

MORDECAI'S REQUEST OF ESTHER'S AID
4:1-17.

4   When Mordecai learned all that had been done, Mordecai rent his clothes and put on sackcloth and ashes, and went out into the midst of the city, wailing with a loud and bitter cry; ²he went up to the entrance of the king's gate, for no one might enter the king's gate clothed with sackcloth. ³And in every province, wherever the king's command and his decree came, there was great mourning among the Jews, with fasting and weeping and lamenting, and most of them lay in sackcloth and ashes.
⁴When Esther's maids and her eunuchs came and told her, the queen was deeply distressed; she sent garments to clothe Mordecai, so that he might take off his sackcloth, but he would not accept them. ⁵Then Esther called for Hathach, one of the king's eunuchs, who had been appointed to attend her, and ordered him to go to Mordecai to learn what this was and why it was. ⁶Hathach went out to Mordecai in the open square of the city in front of the king's gate, ⁷and Mordecai told him all that had happened to him, and the exact sum of money that Haman had promised to pay into the king's treasuries for the destruction of the Jews. ⁸Mordecai also gave him a copy of the written decree issued in Susa for their destruction, that he might show it to Esther and explain it to her and charge her to go to the king to make supplication to him and entreat him for her people. ⁹And Hathach went and told Esther what Mordecai had said. ¹⁰The Esther spoke to Hathach and gave him a message for Mordecai, saying, ¹¹"All the king's servants and the people of the

king's provinces know that if any man or woman goes to the king inside the inner court without being called, there is but one law; all alike are to be put to death, except the one to whom the king holds out the golden scepter that he may live. And I have not been called to come in to the king these thirty days." [12]And they told Mordecai what Esther had said. [13]Then Mordecai told them to return answer to Esther, "Think not that in the king's palace you will escape any more than all the other Jews. [14]For if you keep silence at such a time as this, relief and deliverance will rise for the Jews from another quarter, but you and your father's house will perish. And who knows whether you have not come to the kingdom for such a time as this?" [15]Then Esther told them to reply to Mordecai, [16]"Go, gather all the Jews to be found in Susa, and hold a fast on my behalf, and neither eat nor drink for three days, night or day. I and my maids will also fast as you do. Then I will go to the king, though it is against the law; and if I perish, I perish." [17]Mordecai then went away and did everything as Esther had ordered him.

Mordecai's reaction to the decree is both expected and unexpected. Rending one's clothes, putting on sackcloth, and sprinkling ashes were traditional ways of expressing grief and pain (Gen 37:34; 2 Kgs 18:37). Yet at no time does Mordecai intend these acts as specifically religious. He cries out but not to Yahweh. In the history of Israel fasting was a religious custom (Jer 14:12; Joel 2:12). But for the Jews in the provinces it is not a fast unto the Lord. The author presumably does not intend to downplay the role of God in this crisis. Rather, he chooses to underline the parts to be played by God's own people. In v.14 Mordecai makes the point that even in the event of Esther's silence help will be forthcoming from another source. The author deliberately leaves the phrase vague. He merely wishes to stress the inevitability of some form of help.

The fasting of Esther, her maids, and the Susa Jews in v.16 contrasts with the fasting in the provinces in v.3. The latter expresses resignation, whereas the former contains a glimmer of hope and hence of Esther's success in approaching the king. Though the fast in v.16 avoids mentioning any connection with Jewish faith, it does appear to be more "religiously" oriented than the one in v.3.

At the same time the fasting in chap. 4 contrasts with the feasting which is so typical of the Book of Esther. Esther now fasts but will soon return to feasting in chap. 5. In 2:9 she received special portions from Hegai but now she refuses to eat. The fast is also linked with the feast of Purim. In 9:31 Esther and Mordecai will exercise their royal power in prescribing the feast, just as they earlier called for fasting. The author provides the reader with another contrast: the fasting of chap. 4 will yield to the feasting of chap. 9; the tension of chap. 4 will give way to the resolution of chap. 9.

Mordecai's communication with Esther is another building block in the development of the story. Esther's first proof of concern is to provide clothes for her foster father which he summarily rejects. This rejection then moves the queen to dispatch Hathach to learn the particulars of the dire situation. Mordecai now mentions the intended destruction and intimates its likely outcome by adding Haman's plan to cater to the king's avarice.

A copy of the decree now makes its way to Esther. But the copy is accompanied by Mordecai's demand that Esther intercede with the king on behalf of her people. Mordecai's suggestion reveals the danger surrounding an unsolicited appearance before the king, viz., the death penalty. Although the intended slaughter is still eleven months away, Esther adds that she has not been summoned in thirty days. This prompts Mordecai's observation that Esther too has no special protection by being in the palace. If she remains silent, then she will share the experience of all the Jews. At this Mordecai moves from threats to encouragement. Perhaps her position as queen was intended to meet such a crisis. Esther meets the challenge.

The obedience/disobedience motif is very much in evidence in this chapter. In some respects Mordecai is something of a contradiction. He has refused obeisance to

Haman, yet he now observes the laws with regard to appearing before the king's gate, i.e., the door of the palace. Although he is anxious to consult with Esther, he realizes the obligation of Persian law that one not appear before the king's gate in sackcloth. Ironically, Mordecai is prevented from approaching the royal court, although he has a claim on the king's liberality because of his disclosure of the assassination plot.

Obedience/disobedience also applies to Esther's situation. Both Vashti and Mordecai are parade examples of what can happen if one disobeys the law. But the concern for personal safety must now yield to the common good. Esther's silence will serve no one. It will provide neither for her own personal safety nor for that of her people. The only resolution of the impasse is disobedience. The prohibition not to appear before the king unsummoned may have envisioned the personal safety of the king and the royal family. The reader wonders, however, if her unlawful appearance before Ahasuerus will result in the death penalty. To obey the Persian law may entail death; to disobey the Persian law may entail life for the people. Will Esther fare better than Vashti?

This chapter raises the problem of Jewish identity. Both Esther and Mordecai are willing to accept the consequences for their actions (see v.16). There is a tension here between loyalty to the crown and Jewish solidarity. The author intimates that Jewish solidarity has a greater claim than loyalty to the crown. Yet the distinction is not really so black and white. Actually Jewish loyalty serves the interests of the country, as Esther later explains (7:3-4). Esther's priorities will in the end serve the best interests of the country.

Obviously our author is stating that a good Jew is also a good citizen, because to meet the interests of God's people is not divorced from meeting the good of the empire (see Jer 29:4-7). The fasts in vv.3, 16 already pointed in the direction of Jewish solidarity. Ironically, to fast for the successful outcome of Esther's disobedience (v.16) is really to invite the overthrow of Israel's enemies and therefore Persia's enemies. Though communal solidarity comes first, it also fulfills the best interests of the Persian empire.

Esther is now in charge. In chap. 2 Esther appeared as the obedient foster child of the not so tractable Mordecai. He had commanded her to conceal her Jewish identity (2:10). He also checked up on her during the beauty treatment (2:11). The passage 2:20 provides a picture of the pliable, obliging Hadassah. Even when Mordecai discovers the plot, Esther merely functions as a channel of communication to the king (2:22: "in the name of Mordecai"). In chap. 4 Mordecai is still pursuing his paternal role, insisting that Esther intercede with the king for the Jews. Toward the end of chap. 4 Esther has assumed the role of leader — a role she will not relinquish in the rest of the book. In v.16 she commands Mordecai to gather the Susa Jews for the purpose of fasting. Though Mordecai was responsible for provoking the slaughter, he is in no position to undo the results of his insubordination. Only Esther has any chance of defusing the whole situation. The author clearly indicates this new relationship between Esther and Mordecai when he writes: "Mordecai then went away and did everything as Esther had ordered him" (v.17). Esther is clearly in charge.

The author also links Esther's bold initiative with her role as queen. Esther's royal power was anticipated in 1:19: " 'and let the king give her (Vashti's) royal position to another.' " In the author's view royal power includes not only rights but also obligations. To be ruler means to provide for those ruled. Mordecai suggests this in 4:14 when he reflects: " 'and who knows whether you have not come to the kingdom for such a time as this?' "

Up to this point the abuse of royal power has been more evident than its proper use. Haman the Agagite uses his position to wreak his vengeance upon Mordecai the Saulide — a vengeance which entails the massacre of his people. King Ahasuerus has employed his royal power to suit his own needs: to depose a queen, to institute a beauty contest to find a fitting replacement, to listen to the unscrupulous plot of his prime minister to exterminate part of his empire, and finally to toast the plot in a drinking bout to Susa's amazement. While Ahasuerus appears as a rather weak, acquiescing monarch (so unlike Herodotus' description of Xerxes I), Esther will demonstrate the very purpose of royal power, viz., to provide for others, especially the disenfranchised.

ESTHER'S MACHINATIONS
5:1-14.

Esther now undertakes to save her people. At the same time Haman initiates a further plot against Mordecai. The material may be divided as follows: (1) Esther's audience with the king and her first banquet (5:1-8); (2) Haman's plot against Mordecai (5:9-14).

ESTHER'S AUDIENCE WITH THE KING AND HER FIRST BANQUET
5:1-8.

5 On the third day Esther put on her royal robes and stood in the inner court of the king's palace, opposite the king's hall. The king was sitting on his royal throne inside the palace opposite the entrance to the palace; [2]and when the king saw Queen Esther standing in the court, she found favor in his sight and he held out to Esther the golden scepter that was in his hand. Then Esther approached and touched the top of the scepter. [3]And the king said to her, "What is it, Queen Esther? What is your request? It shall be given you, even to the half of my kingdom." [4]And Esther said, "If it please the king, let the king and Haman come this day to a dinner that I have prepared for the king." [5]Then said the king, "Bring

Haman quickly, that we may do as Esther desires." So the king and Haman came to the dinner that Esther had prepared. ⁶And as they were drinking wine, the king said to Esther, "What is your petition? It shall be granted you. And what is your request? Even to the half of my kingdom, it shall be fulfilled." ⁷But Esther said, "My petition and my request is: ⁸If I have found favor in the sight of the king, and if it please the king to grant my petition and fulfil my request, let the king and Haman come tomorrow to the dinner which I will prepare for them, and tomorrow I will do as the king has said."

In 4:14 Mordecai had raised the question whether Esther had become queen at this particular time because of the Jewish crisis. In answer to that question the author has Esther play the role of queen to the extreme. In v.1 the Hebrew word for "kingship" appears three times; the Hebrew word for "king" also appears three times. The author is suggesting that the resolution of the crisis may hinge on the royal position of the heroine.

In this connection the motif of banquet is once again significant. Esther plays the royal hostess: first to Ahasuerus who is also to bring Haman along, secondly to Ahasuerus and Haman as somewhat coequal guests. Just as the banquets in chap. 1 proved to be the downfall of Vashti, it is at least possible that these banquets could also go awry. At the same time the reader is aware that banquets are linked to disempowering influential people. Thus, Haman may also go the way of Vashti.

Suspense is uppermost in the mind of the author. In v.4, when Esther has her chance to reply to the king's request and thus avert the slaughter of her people, the coy queen chooses to delay and recommends the first banquet. On the occasion of this banquet, when the king again presses the question, the queen recommends the second banquet. At this point the reader is becoming uneasy. Will the king's patience continue? Even if Esther can avert the disaster which threatens her people, will she still be able to save Mordecai? Given the king's all-consuming love for Esther, the reader may presume that the king will continue to be patient. However, given the interminable delays, Mordecai's fate hangs limply in the balance.

Esther's character begins to emerge with greater clarity. The fast which she prescribed for the Jews of Susa, her maidens, and herself now gives way to her striking appearance in royal robes. Esther has assumed center stage — a position that she will relinquish to no one, including Ahasuerus, Haman, and Mordecai. Although her switch from the obedient foster child to strong-willed queen was indicated at the end of chap. 4, that change is more in evidence in chap. 5. Esther chooses to disregard the law of appearing before the king unsummoned, although the penalty is death. The reader begins to assume that the king's love will surpass the disobedience. Yet it is more the self-assurance of the queen rather than the generosity of the king which brings about the all-forgiving touch of the golden scepter. The fate of the Jewish nation is bound up with the daring of the queen. Her boldness offers more than a passing expression of hope that it will be the queen who will resolve the question and defuse the explosive situation.

HAMAN'S PLOT AGAINST MORDECAI
5:9-14.

9And Haman went out that day joyful and glad of heart. But when Haman saw Mordecai in the king's gate, that he neither rose nor trembled before him, he was filled with wrath against Mordecai. 10Nevertheless Haman restrained himself, and went home; and he sent and fetched his friends and his wife Zeresh. 11And Haman recounted to them the splendor of his riches, the number of his sons, all the promotions with which the king had honored him, and how he had advanced him above the princes and the servants of the king. 12And Haman added, "Even Queen Esther let no one come with the king to the banquet she prepared but myself. And tomorrow also I am invited by her together with the king. 13Yet all this does me no good, so long as I see Mordecai the Jew sitting at the king's gate." [14]Then his wife Zeresh and all his friends said to him, "Let a gallows fifty cubits high be made, and in the morning tell the king to have Mordecai hanged upon it; then go merrily with the king to the dinner." This counsel pleased Haman and he had the gallows made.

Haman continues his paranoid character. Even after the consoling experience of the first banquet, Haman is still unable to cope with Mordecai. Whereas previously Mordecai had refused to bow down (3:2), he now refuses to rise at the appearance of the prime minister. He is indeed able to restrain himself but the restraint seems to be wearing thin. At the meeting with his wife and friends he recounts his wealth, his family, and his climb up the diplomatic ladder. The pinnacle of success is clearly the forthcoming banquet. Yet all this goes for nothing since Mordecai continues to haunt him.

His wife's suggestion to construct a gallows seventy-five feet high will apparently resolve the issue once and for all. But in having the gallows constructed, Haman must admit two points. First of all, Mordecai is more than an insignificant character since a gallows of such height is suited only for a person of high rank. Secondly, Haman has no permission to erect the gallows. Once again he has acted prematurely. One wonders if both acts of disobedience, viz., the plan to exterminate the Jews and the erection of the gallows, will somehow backfire. The author slyly notes that the Jews may exterminate others and that someone other than Mordecai will face the gallows. Obedience/disobedience is again at work.

MORDECAI'S VINDICATION
6:1-13.

Before resolving the crisis facing the Jewish people, the author resolves the crisis facing Mordecai. The king becomes aware of his previous loyalty and with the approval of Haman proceeds to reward the faithful Jew. The author also suggests the demise of Haman himself.

6 On that night the king could not sleep; and he gave orders to bring the book of memorable deeds, the chronicles, and they were read before the king. ²And it was found written how Mordecai had told about Bigthana and Teresh, two of the king's eunuchs, who guarded the threshold, and who had sought to lay hands upon King Ahasuerus. ³And the king said, "What honor or dignity has been bestowed on Mordecai for this?" The king's servants who attended him said, "Nothing has been done for him." ⁴And the king said, "Who is in the court?" Now Haman had just entered the outer court of the king's palace to speak to the king about having Mordecai hanged on the gallows that he had prepared for him. ⁵So the king's servants told him, "Haman is there, standing in the court." And the king said, "Let him come in." ⁶So Haman came in, and the king said to him, "What shall be done to the man whom the king delights to honor?" And Haman said to himself, "Whom would the king delight to honor more than me?" ⁷And Haman said to the king,

"For the man whom the king delights to honor, [8]let royal robes be brought, which the king has worn, and the horse which the king has ridden, and on whose head a royal crown is set; [9]and let the robes and the horse be handed over to one of the king's most noble princes; let him array the man whom the king delights to honor, and let him conduct the man on horseback through the open square of the city, proclaiming before him: 'Thus shall it be done to the man whom the king delights to honor.'" [10]Then the king said to Haman, "Make haste, take the robes and the horse, as you have said, and do so to Mordecai the Jew who sits at the king's gate. Leave out nothing that you have mentioned." [11]So Haman took the robes and the horse, and he arrayed Mordecai and made him ride through the open square of the city, proclaiming, "Thus shall it be done to the man whom the king delights to honor."

[12]Then Mordecai returned to the king's gate. But Haman hurried to his house, mourning and with his head covered. [13]And Haman told his wife Zeresh and all his friends everything that had befallen him. Then his wise men and his wife Zeresh said to him, "If Mordecai, before whom you have begun to fall, is of the Jewish people, you will not prevail against him but will surely fall before him."

The author of Esther was certainly familiar with the story of Joseph. A comparison of Gen 41:42-43 with Esth 6:11; 8:2 bears this out. "Then Pharaoh *took his signet ring* from his hand and *put it on Joseph's hand,* and *arrayed* him in garments of fine linen, and put a gold chain about his neck; and he *made him to ride* in his second chariot, and *they cried before him,* 'Bow the knee!'" (Gen 41:42-43). "So Haman took the robes and the horse, and he *arrayed* Mordecai and *made him ride* through the open square of the city, *proclaiming, . . .* (6:11). "and the king *took off his signet ring,* which he had taken from Haman, and *gave it to Mordecai"* (8:2).

Besides these linguistic parallels, there are other resemblances. Thus, the Joseph story also refers to the two eunuchs who had offended the king (see Gen 40:1-3). Joseph's relationship with the eunuchs (Gen 40:4-23) and Pharaoh's restless sleep (Gen 41:1) are also significant factors in Joseph's climb to fame and fortune.

There are also differences. When Pharaoh honors Joseph, he immediately sets him over all of Egypt (Gen 41:43). When Ahasuerus honors Mordecai, he does not place him over the Persian Empire immediately. Moreover, Pharaoh's dream is not the same as Ahasuerus' insomnia. While the author of Esther used the Joseph story to advantage, he did not imitate it slavishly.

The motifs of royal power and obedience/disobedience are again paramount. Although the prime minister enjoys power, he usurps royal power by constructing the gallows before obtaining the necessary permission. It is not surprising that those who employ royal power for the common good (Esther and Mordecai) are vindicated, while those who manipulate it for personal gain (Haman) are disgraced.

It is not clear who wears the royal crown in v.8, i.e., the horse or Mordecai. In either case it is a conferral of royal honor. Similarly, to wear the royal robes is more than a gesture on Ahasuerus' part. The dress implies royal power and anticipates Mordecai's elevation to prime minister. The clothes make the man — here a king. Esther's donning the royal crown in 2:17 looked to the use of royal power. The same is to be expected in Mordecai's case. Unlike Vashti, neither Esther nor Mordecai refuses the crown. The reader is indeed straining to learn the implications of such power for the crisis at hand.

The return of Mordecai and Haman in vv. 12-13 is a study in contrasts. Although Mordecai's promotion is still pending, he does return to his position at court ("to the king's gate"). The author refuses to describe the return as a triumph, but he suggests that by painting a rather dour picture of Haman. He is clearly in pain. Both the mourning and the covered head, a sign of grief (see Jer 14:3-4; Ezek 24:17), reveal a crestfallen Haman. Significantly Haman's return home is always court related. Once again he confers with his wife and friends, the very ones who suggested the gallows for Mordecai. Given Mordecai's ethnic origin, Haman learns their verdict, viz., that he cannot prevail. Perhaps the banquet to which he is whisked off in v.14 will resolve matters!

The irony continues. A scene similar to David and Nathan in 2 Sam 12:1-7 (see also 2 Sam 14:1-17), where the guilty party unwittingly implicates himself, now unfolds between Ahasuerus and Haman. Thinking that the king will honor him (" 'Whom else would the king delight to honor more than me?' "), Haman is thus set up. He proffers all the fitting signs of honor and respect only to learn that Mordecai, not himself, has won the day. To add to the situation, Haman himself must faithfully execute all the suggestions he has made to the king (" 'Leave out nothing that you have mentioned.' "). Previously Mordecai had refused to bow down and rise at the approach of Haman. Now Haman must lead Mordecai through the city and show proper respect to the very man who had refused him respect.

The author converses with his readers. He chooses to omit certain details in order to entertain the audience and sustain the suspense. Thus, in leading Mordecai through the city, the author does not mention Haman's reactions but prefers to let the reader imagine them. In v.10 the author does not explain how the king knows that Mordecai is a Jew. He does not raise the question whether somehow Mordecai will escape the fate of his co-religionists. The author trusts his audience. In turn, the audience is asked to trust the author and await the not too distant denouement.

Are all these happenings merely chance? Is it by chance that the king suffers from insomnia (see Dan 6:19) and thus has the opportunity to learn of Mordecai's unrewarded act of loyalty? Is it by chance that Haman arrives on the scene at the very moment when the king seeks the proper way to honor Mordecai? For the author there is no great implausibility in any of the events. He refuses to use the word "providence" or mention the name of the God of Israel explicitly. In the other direction, he allows humans to occupy center stage. The answer would seem to be that it is not chance that determines the outcome but the persistent, dogged efforts of people such as Esther and Mordecai.

Nationalism emerges once again. Verse 10 again identifies Mordecai as a Jew. However, the new element is the apparent inviolability of the Jews as expressed by Zeresh and friends: " 'If Mordecai, before whom you have begun to fall, is of the Jewish people, you will not prevail against him but will surely fall before him' " (v.13). This nationalism goes hand in hand with the coincidences mentioned above. The author is laboring to say that Jews who stick together and value their heritage even to the point of civil disobedience will eventually win out. At the same time the good Jew can also be a loyal, law-abiding citizen of a foreign power. While Esther and Mordecai are parade examples of civil disobedience, they are also the exemplars of loyalty to the state. Ironically, by recognizing national (hence religious) identity as their priority, they are in a position to promote the welfare of the empire. The Jews of the Persian Diaspora can be both good Jews and good Persians.

ESTHER'S FURTHER MACHINATIONS AND THEIR SUCCESS 6:14-8:17.

The author now deals with the second banquet given by Esther. Its success leads to the demise of Haman and the exoneration of Mordecai. The stage is now set for undoing the extermination of the Jews by issuing a second royal decree. The material may be divided as follows: (1) Esther's second banquet (6:14-7:10); (2) Mordecai's exoneration (8:1-2); (3) the second royal decree (8:3-17).

ESTHER'S SECOND BANQUET 6:14-7:10.

14While they were yet talking with him, the king's eunuchs arrived and brought Haman in haste to the banquet that Esther had prepared.
7 So the king and Haman went in to feast with Queen Esther. 2And on the second day, as they were drinking wine, the king again said to Esther, "What is your petition, Queen Esther? It shall be granted you. And what is your request? Even to the half of my kingdom, it shall be fulfilled." 3Then Queen Esther answered, "If I have found favor in your sight, O king, and if it please the king, let my life be given me at my petition, and my people at my request. 4For we are sold, I and my people, to be

destroyed, to be slain, and to be annihilated. If we had been sold merely as slaves, men and women, I would have held my peace; for our affliction is not to be compared with the loss to the king." ⁵Then King Ahasuerus said to Queen Esther, "Who is he, and where is he, that would presume to do this?" ⁶And Esther said, "A foe and enemy! This wicked Haman!" Then Haman was in terror before the king and the queen. ⁷And the king rose from the feast in wrath and went into the palace garden; but Haman stayed to beg his life from Queen Esther, for he saw that evil was determined against him by the king. ⁸And the king returned from the palace garden to the place where they were drinking wine, as Haman was falling on the couch where Esther was; and the king said, "Will he even assault the queen in my presence, in my own house?" As the words left the mouth of the king, they covered Haman's face. ⁹Then said Harbona, one of the eunuchs in attendance on the king, "Moreover, the gallows which Haman has prepared for Mordecai, whose word saved the king, is standing in Haman's house, fifty cubits high." ¹⁰And the king said, "Hang him on that." So they hanged Haman on the gallows which he had prepared for Mordecai. Then the anger of the king abated.

The banquet motif returns and the reader is not totally surprised at the demise of Haman. Banquets are calculated to bring about both demise and promotion. The first banquet hosted by Esther was a rather enjoyable occasion which prompted the second banquet. On this occasion, however, the enjoyable atmosphere dissipates as the showdown between Esther and Haman approaches. There hangs in the balance the fateful decree issued in the king's name ordering the execution of the Jews

Instead of smoke-filled backrooms Persian politics are concluded in an atmosphere of banqueting. One instinctively thinks of Queen Vashti and the king's second banquet. The banquet provided the occasion for Vashti's disobedience and subsequent deposing which in turn provided the occasion for Esther's rise. (In both the deposing of Vashti [2:1] and the demise of Haman [7:10] the text notes that the anger of the king abated.) Esther's second banquet thus serves as the foil for disempowering Haman and thereby effecting the salvation of the Jewish population. Banquets are a necessary ingredient of the political machine. A Judaism without banquets and politics is hardly a viable Judaism.

For the third time Ahasuerus poses his twofold question: what is your petition? what is your request? The reader recalls immediately the apparent snubbing of the king in 5:3-6. But it is not really a snubbing since the author has chosen to heighten the tension, suggesting that the third time will release the tension. Given the situation of grave peril to the Jewish people and granted the Jewishness of the queen, one wonders if she will gather the necessary courage to confront Haman by accepting the challenge of the king's question. At the same time the twofold question anticipates 9:12. When the king asks about the Jews in Susa and their self-defensive war, Esther is once again up to the challenge. She persuades the king to prolong the war in Susa from the 13th to the 14th of Adar. The question presupposes both Esther's influence over the king and her concern for the Jewish people. Her answer consolidates both aspects.

Will the real Haman please stand up? Haman has come off as a sly, conceited politician interested in his own good rather than the common good. One looks forward to the moment when the real Haman will be unmasked and thus forced to stand up. Chap. 7 offers the opportunity to discover the devious character of the prime minister.

Most likely 3:9-11 was a deception on Haman's part to win over the king and wreak his revenge on Mordecai and the Jewish people. In promising to contribute 10,000 talents to the king's treasury, Haman had duped the king into thinking that the financial gain would result from enslaving the Jews, not exterminating them. Esther's reply in v.4 appears to support this view, although the verse is perhaps the most difficult in the entire book. The expression "to be sold" reinforces the view that the prime minister wanted the king to think only in terms of slavery. The noun "slaves" is perhaps a play on words in Hebrew related to 3:9 ("cause to become homeless" rather than the RSV "to be destroyed").

The force of v.4 is, therefore, that Esther would not have bothered the king, if it were merely a question of slavery rather than extermination. The king's reaction in v.5 is due, not only to his love for the queen, but also to the machinations of the prime minister. It is now apparent that Haman was interested in personal gain all along and not the good of the king and empire.

Loyalty is again a primary concern of the author. Esther would have remained silent, if Haman's plot involved only enslavement. However, annihilation is directly opposed to the best interests of the king and the nation. In identifying herself, Esther bound up her personal fate with that of her people: " '. . . my life . . . , and my people . . . For we are sold, I and my people' "). In thus opting for the welfare of her people, Esther has thereby opted for the welfare of the state. A loyal Jew can also be a loyal Persian. A persecutor of Jews can also be a disloyal Persian. To add to the charges against Haman, Harbona notes that he not only deceived the king but even attempted to hurt the king's benefactor, i.e., Mordecai. Jewish loyalty to the crown is irrefutable.

The element of irony is not lacking in chap. 7. In 3:2 Mordecai refused to bow down to Haman; in 5:9 he did not rise for Haman. In 7:7 Haman stayed to beg for his life. Literally "he stood." In 7:8 he was falling on Esther's couch. Haman is now involved in the very actions which Mordecai had refused him. The man who sought to annihilate the Jews must plead for his life from a Jewess. Indeed, the irony continues when the king returns at the very moment that Haman is falling on Esther's couch. The charge of attempted rape and treason is the result of the seemingly fortuitous arrival. Finally the very means which Haman had contrived to kill Mordecai becomes his own undoing. Prov 26:26 is an apt commentary: "He who digs a pit will fall into it, and a stone will come back upon him who starts it rolling."

Chap. 7 is added proof that Esther is fully in command. She has emerged as a strong-willed monarch who places a higher value on religious loyalty but at the same time supports the common good. The author demonstrates the queen's determination by omitting any reply on her part to Haman's request for mercy. Esther appears, not so much ruthless as determined, not so much pitiless as inflexible. She will not yield when the good of her people and the good of her nation are in jeopardy. Whereas Haman is conniving and the king is vacillating, Esther follows the inexorable course dictated by the needs of the moment. She is not only a queen. She is an admirable leader.

MORDECAI'S EXONERATION
8:1-2.

8 On that day King Ahasuerus gave to Queen Esther the house of Haman, the enemy of the Jews. And Mordecai came before the king, for Esther had told what he was to her; [2]and the king took off his signet ring, which he had taken from Haman, and gave it to Mordecai. And Esther set Mordecai over the house of Haman.

Long live the new prime minister! Like Joseph, Mordecai occupies the second most important position in the empire. Mordecai's pardon in chap. 6 now gives way to exoneration by coronation. The suggested royal status of chap. 6 becomes a reality. It is now clear that he wears a crown and is decked out in royal robes. The former insignificant civil servant now gives orders and others must obey.

In v.1 Esther explains to Ahasuerus her relationship to Mordecai. In v.7 Mordecai is labelled "Mordecai the Jew." The word "Jew" no longer has the ring of disloyalty or suspicion. Indeed, to call Haman "the enemy of the Jews" is now to imply that he is the real enemy of the state. The author's audience must have reveled in the fact that one of their own — like biblical Joseph — could make it all the way to the top. At the same time that audience also perceived that to promote the cause of Judaism need not run counter

to the cause of the empire. Mordecai was the very embodiment of the fact that the Diaspora Jew could also serve his
God by serving a foreign power.

The author does not allow his readers to forget that it is a
woman who is responsible for Mordecai's new position.
Hadassah, the former ward of Mordecai, is now the queen
and it is her turn to control the destiny of her cousin. Since
Haman was guilty of treason, his property reverted to the
crown. In a gesture of concern for his troubled wife
Ahasuerus turns Haman's property over to Esther who in
turn gives it to Mordecai. Secondly, Esther explained her
relationship to Mordecai, to the king. It is only after this
explanation that the king makes Mordecai the prime
minister. Esther has emerged as more than a beauty contest
winner. She reflects concern for her people as a whole and
for her cousin in particular. Queenship has implied reaching
out, even at the risk of personal loss. The lady in charge does
not neglect her charges.

THE SECOND ROYAL DECREE
8:3-17.

[3]Then Esther spoke again to the king; she fell at his feet
and besought him with tears to avert the evil design of
Haman the Agagite and the plot which he had devised
against the Jews. [4]And the king held out the golden
scepter to Esther, [5]and Esther rose and stood before the
king. And she said, "If it please the king, and if I have
found favor in his sight, and if the thing seem right before
the king, and I be pleasing in his eyes, let an order be
written to revoke the letters devised by Haman the
Agagite, the son of Ham-medatha, which he wrote to
destroy the Jews who are in all the provinces of the king.
[6]For how can I endure to see the calamity that is coming
to my people? Or how can I endure to see the destruction
of my kindred?" [7]Then King Ahasuerus said to Queen
Esther and to Mordecai the Jew, "Behold, I have given
Esther the house of Haman, and they have hanged him on

the gallows, because he would lay hands on the Jews. [8]And you may write as you please with regard to the Jews, in the name of the king, and seal it with the king's ring; for an edict written in the name of the king and sealed with the king's ring cannot be revoked."

[9]The king's secretaries were summoned at that time, in the third month, which is the month of Sivan, on the twenty-third day; and an edict was written according to all that Mordecai commanded concerning the Jews to the satraps and the governors and the princes of the provinces from India to Ethiopia, a hundred and twenty-seven provinces, to every province in its own script and to every people in its own language, and also to the Jews in their script and their language. [10]The writing was in the name of King Ahasuerus and sealed with the king's ring, and letters were sent by mounted couriers riding on swift horses that were used in the king's service, bred from the royal stud. [11]By these the king allowed the Jews who were in every city to gather and defend their lives, to destroy, to slay, and to annihilate any armed force of any people or province that might attack them, with their children and women, and to plunder their goods, [12]upon one day throughout all the provinces of King Ahasuerus, on the thirteenth day of the twelfth month, which is the month of Adar. [13]A copy of what was written was to be issued as a decree in every province, and by proclamation to all peoples, and the Jews were to be ready on that day to avenge themselves upon their enemies. [14]So the couriers, mounted on their swift horses that were used in the king's service, rode out in haste, urged by the king's command; and the decree was issued in Susa the capital.

[15]Then Mordecai went out from the presence of the king in royal robes of blue and white, with a great golden crown and a mantle of fine linen and purple, while the city of Susa shouted and rejoiced. [16]The Jews had light and gladness and joy and honor. [17]And in every province and in every city, wherever the king's command and his edict came, there was gladness and joy among the Jews, a feast and a holiday. And many from the peoples of the country declared themselves Jews, for the fear of the Jews had fallen upon them.

While Mordecai's safety is assured, the fate of the Jews as a whole is questionable. Unfortunately the decree is still in force. In order to avert disaster, Esther employs all her court etiquette and adds her own unique charm as well. She falls at the king's feet and weeps on behalf of her people. (The king's gesture with the golden scepter does not necessarily mean that Esther has approached the king unsummoned.) After the proper social graces in v.5 Esther supplies the following personal dimension which is certain to win the king over: " '. . . and (if) I be pleasing in his eyes, let an order be written to revoke the letters . . .' " Coming as it does at the end of v.5, this addition is calculated to reinforce the revocation of the decree. Moreover, the vocabulary of v.6 enhances her plea. "Calamity" and "destruction" are exceedingly plaintive on the lips of the queen.

There is an obvious touch of irony regarding the revocation of the decree. According to 1:19 the laws of the Persians and the Medes cannot be revoked. In v.8 Ahasuerus permits Esther and Mordecai to write whatever they please regarding the Jews. He allows them to undo the first decree but then adds: " 'for an edict written in the name of the king and sealed with the king's ring cannot be revoked.' " To suggest change and then to observe the impossibility of the change is indeed ironical.

The decree in vv.9-14 is similar to the first decree in 3:12-15a. The phrase "to destroy, to slay, and to annihilate all Jews" (3:13 and used by Esther in 7:4) reappears in v.11 but with a different object, viz., all those attacking the Jews. The tables have been turned. A first reaction is to concentrate on the unmitigated slaughter which embraces women and children. The author's approach, however, is not to endorse or condemn such slaughter, but simply to announce the reversal in the category of the enemy. The former enemy, the Jews, has now received the blessing of the state to wage a defensive war. The author is implying that only fools would dare to engage the Jews in combat since a royal decree now allows them not only to kill but also to plunder. The Jews of the empire are now a force to be reckoned with. To disregard the decree is to invite disaster.

The author is at pains to point out the differences in the two decrees. In v.9 there is the additional note of the 127 provinces (1:1). Moreover, the Jews are now included among the recipients of the decree "in their script and language." In dispatching the decree, special royal horses are used. Although Aramaic was the "lingua franca" of the empire, the references to the script and language of every province are the author's means of stressing the importance of the communication. In the first decree the provinces had eleven months' advance warning about the intended slaughter of the Jews. In the second decree the provinces have approximately nine months' advance warning about the intended slaughter of the non-Jews. Clearly the second decree is much more elaborate. It is evidence that the Jews in the persons of Esther and Mordecai have gained an upper hand.

The writing of the decree also signals a significant change in power. Although written and sealed in the king's name, the second decree is the work of Esther and Ahasuerus. Verse 9 emphasizes: "and an edict was written to all that Mordecai commanded." The royal power of both Esther and Mordecai is not limited to their crowns and apparel. It is evident in their issuing a decree which will provide for the well-being of their people. To dictate decrees is to be in charge. The very people once threatened by an imperial decree now has its own in high places who are responsible for the new decree.

The reaction of both the Jews and the pagans is a telling element in the chapter. In 3:15 when Ahasuerus and Haman sat down to toast the destruction of the Jews, the city of Susa was thrown into confusion. In v.15 when Mordecai appears in all the trappings of his new office, "the city of Susa shouted and rejoiced." Previously the Jews were the enemies of the state, but now they enjoy "light and gladness and joy and honor" (v.16). In reaction to the second decree many of the pagans (v.17) become converts to Judaism. The hated Jews are now drawing more than passing attention.

According to v.17 the reason for the conversions is that the fear of the Jews had fallen upon the pagans. A comparatively small number of people out of the immense Persian Empire are now such that they can command the fear of the general populace and even move them to join their religious ranks.

The feasting motif is a good commentary on the reversal of fortunes. In 4:3 the Jews in the provinces began to fast because of the first decree. Now at the arrival of the second decree a holiday spirit takes over (v.17). Ahasuerus' second banquet provoked the deposing of Vashti and the emergence of Esther. Esther's second banquet led to the demise of Haman and the rise of Mordecai. This Jewish feasting is linked to the earlier banquets. While it celebrates the newly acquired powers of Esther and Mordecai, it also looks to the feast of Purim and another banquet to celebrate the Jewish victory in Susa and the provinces. Feasting connotes disempowering the incumbents and empowering the new candidates. To feast is to savor the sweet taste of victory.

THE FEAST OF PURIM
9:1-32.

The author narrates the account of the Jewish victory over the pagans in Susa and the provinces. The chapter concludes with details and background for the feast of Purim. The material may be divided as follows: (1) the Jewish victory (9:1-19); (2) the feast of Purim (9:20-32).

THE JEWISH VICTORY
9:1-19.

9 Now in the twelfth month, which is the month of Adar, on the thirteenth day of the same, when the king's command and edict were about to be executed, on the very day when the enemies of the Jews hoped to get the mastery over them, but which had been changed to a day when the Jews should get mastery over their foes, ²the Jews gathered in their cities throughout all the provinces of King Ahasuerus to lay hands on such as sought their hurt. And no one could make a stand against them, for the fear of them had fallen upon all peoples. ³All the princes of the provinces and the satraps and the governors and the royal officials also helped the Jews, for the fear of Mordecai had fallen upon them. ⁴For Mordecai was great in the king's house, and his fame spread throughout all the provinces; for the man Mordecai grew more and more powerful. ⁵So the Jews smote all their enemies with the sword, slaughtering, and destroying them, and did as they pleased to those who hated them. ⁶In Susa the capital itself the Jews slew and destroyed five hundred men, ⁷and also slew Parshandatha and Dalphon and Aspatha ⁸and Poratha and Adalia and Aridatha ⁹and Parmashta and Arisai and Aridai and Vaizatha, ¹⁰the ten sons of Haman the son of Hammedatha, the enemy of the Jews; but they laid no hand on the plunder.

¹¹That very day the number of those slain in Susa the capital was reported to the king. ¹²And the king said to Queen Esther, "In Susa the capital the Jews have slain five hundred men and also the ten sons of Haman. What then have they done in the rest of the king's provinces! Now what is your petition? It shall be granted you. And what further is your request? It shall be fulfilled." ¹³And Esther said,"If it please the king, let the Jews who are in Susa be allowed tomorrow also to do according to this day's edict. And let the ten sons of Haman be hanged on the gallows." ¹⁴So the king commanded this to be done; a decree was issued in Susa, and the ten sons of Haman were hanged. ¹⁵The Jews who were in Susa gathered also on the fourteenth day of the month of Adar and they slew three hundred men in Susa; but they laid no hands on the plunder.

¹⁶Now the other Jews who were in the king's provinces also gathered to defend their lives, and got relief from their enemies, and slew seventy-five thousand of those who hated them; but they laid no hands on the plunder. ¹⁷This was on the thirteenth day of the Month of Adar, and on the fourteenth day they rested and made that a day of feasting and gladness. ¹⁸But the Jews who were in Susa gathered on the thirteenth day and on the fourteenth, and rested on the fifteenth day, making that day of feasting and gladness. ¹⁹Therefore the Jews of the villages, who live in the open towns, hold the fourteenth day of the month of Adar as a day for gladness and a day on month of Adar as a day for gladness and feasting and holiday-making, a day on which they send choice portions to one another.

The killing of 75,800 people has created no little difficulty for commentators. According to v.5 the Jews were empowered to act "as they pleased." The words of the same verse bear out the apparent carte blanche: "smote . . . with the sword, slaughtering, and destroying them. . ." Upon receiving the casualty report of those killed in the Susa acropolis (not the capital), the king relays the message to Esther and conjectures: "'What then have they done in the rest of the king's provinces!'" However, the author mentions three times (vv.10, 15-16) that the Jews did not plunder. Rather than be appalled at the casualty figures, one should inquire into the author's way of telling the story. After all, he wrote the story and he did it his way. However, to understand his point of view does not mean to subscribe to such methods today. The modern audience of Esther enjoys the interaction of the ongoing Word of God.

Humor is not wanting in the telling of the story. According to the second decree the Jews were empowered to kill all those "that might attack them" (8:11). Hence, if the enemy did not attack, the Jews would not be forced to defend themselves. Given these circumstances, who would be so foolish as to incur the wrath of the Jews and thus invite death? The casualty figures indicate that 800 in Susa and 75,000 in the provinces were that stupid! This is not the first time that the author has poked fun at non-Jews. Moreover, v.6 relates the casualty figures for the acropolis and adds the list of Haman's ten sons. The repetition of the report in v.11 is deliberate. Granted the success in Susa, the king can only wonder how many more of his subjects will be killed in the provinces. Instead of showing any displeasure, he merely proceeds to ask the queen about her most recent petition.

The mention of not plundering reflects the Saulide-Amalekite feud discussed earlier. In 1 Sam 15 King Saul and his troops disobeyed the rules of the holy war and plundered the Amalekites. As a result, King Saul was to lose his crown. Here, however, the situation is reversed. The Jews refrain from plundering and thus remove all the stigma attached to the family tree. Mordecai thereby continues to retain his royal power.

The tables have been turned (at the end of v.1 read: "the situation was changed: the Jews got mastery over their foes") but Yahweh is not mentioned explicitly. Rather, the overwhelming Jewish victory is due to their prowess and determination. By dint of royal maneuvers the Jews have clearly gained the upper hand. Fear of the Jews (8:17) reappears in this chapter (v.2). Although under a foreign power, actually the greatest power of the Near East, the Jews are capable of inspiring dread in their opponents. It is not a return to the days of the Davidic monarchy; it is simply the fact of nationalistic effort without benefit of their own king. Ironically, they gain support from Persian bureaucrats (v.3) but ostensibly not from Yahweh. This is surprising since v.27 refers to the Jewish converts. Thus, subjects of the Persian crown become Jews but their allegiance to Yahweh is not stated.

Elsewhere (2:5) the author had mentioned a link with pre-exilic Israel. Moreover, the Saulide-Amalekite feud implies such a link as well. One cannot escape the impression that their national identity presupposes religious identity and thus Yahweh is very much in control of the situation, although in a most subdued but real way, as he works through the leaders of the people. Ultimately the Jews in the book are redefining their concept of election. To thrive in the Diaspora is also a sign of God's choice of Israel. To be a loyal Jew does not necessarily entail living in the Promised Land. Though the Diaspora has its dangers, it also has its advantages, as Esther, Mordecai, and the community have demonstrated. The Book of Esther rejects the closed-door policy of the reforming Nehemiah. Identity does not depend on geography.

The banqueting of chap. 9 binds the entire book together. In chap. 1 Ahasuerus hosted two banquets: the first for officials from the various Persian provinces and the second for the inhabitants of Susa. Similarly, according to 9:17-18, the celebration of Purim on the 14th of Adar is for all the provinces whereas the feast of the 15th of Adar is for the Susa Jews. On the other hand, Ahasuerus held his banquets only once while the Jewish celebrations take place each year.

The character of the Purim celebrations is clearly one of joy. According to vv.17-18 the Jews rest and have a day of feasting and gladness. According to v.19 it is a day "for gladness and feasting and holiday-making, and . . . choice portions" (see also v.22). Now that the author has resolved the tension of the royal decrees, a festal mood seems to be the only appropriate way to react. To celebrate the joy of Purim is to be caught up in the anxiety of oppression and yet the joy of victory. It is not without reason that vv.21, 28 emphasize the need of annual remembrance. The joy of the original event becomes a contagious experience for the Jews, especially those in the Diaspora. Through the celebration the joy continues to exert a force.

Esther plays a significant role in vv.11-14. The petition and request of v.12 recall the king's question in 5:3, 6; 7:2. By this time the reader has no doubt but that the king will more than graciously accede to the queen's wishes. The wish is twofold: the extension of the defensive war for an extra day in Susa and the hanging of Haman's ten sons. Because of this wish some consider Esther nothing more than a bloodthirsty Jael (see Judg 4:17-22). But this seems to miss the author's point. For his audience, not necessarily today's audience, Esther must identify in terms of the common good in precisely this way.

THE FEAST OF PURIM
9:20-32.

20And Mordecai recorded these things, and sent letters to all the Jews who were in all the provinces of King Ahasuerus, both near and far, 21enjoining them that they should keep the fourteenth day of the month of Adar and also the fifteenth day of the same, year by year, 22as the days on which the Jews got relief from their enemies, and as the month that had been turned for them from sorrow into gladness and from mourning into a holiday; that they should make them days of feasting and gladness, days for sending choice portions to one another and gifts to the poor.

23So the Jews undertook to do as they had begun, and as Mordecai had written to them. 24For Haman the Agagite, the son of Hammedatha, the enemy of all the Jews, had plotted against the Jews to destroy them, and had cast Pur, that is the lot, to crush and destroy them; 25but when Esther came before the king, he gave orders in writing that his wicked plot which he had devised against the Jews should come upon his own head, and that he and his sons should be hanged on the gallows. 26Therefore they called these days Purim, after the term Pur. And therefore, because of all that was written in this letter, and of what they had faced in this matter, and of what had befallen them, 27the Jews ordained and took it upon themselves and their descendants and all who joined them, that without fail they would keep these two days according to what was written and at the time appointed every year, 28that these days should be remembered and kept throughout every generation, in every family, province, and city, and that these days of Purim should never fall into disuse among the Jews, nor should the commemoration of these days cease among their descendants.

29Then Queen Esther, the daughter of Abihail, and Mordecai the Jew gave full written authority, confirming this second letter about Purim. 30Letters were sent to all the Jews, to the hundred and twenty-seven provinces of the kingdom of Ahasuerus, in words of peace and truth, 31that these days of Purim should be observed at their appointed seasons, as Mordecai the Jew and Queen Esther enjoined upon the Jews, and as they had laid down for themselves and for their descendants, with regard to their fasts and their lamenting. 32The command of Queen Esther fixed these practices of Purim, and it was recorded in writing.

The origins of the feast of Purim are obscure. A likely solution is that the origins must be traced to several civilizations. The word itself *(pūru)* is a Babylonian word meaning "lot." However, it then becomes the name of a Jewish feast which began in the communities of the eastern Diaspora. Ironically, the feast is not a religious feast like Passover or Tabernacles. It has no cultic elements and is not bound up with the traditional sacred history of the Chosen People. Moreover, Purim derives from a book which in the Hebrew text does not even mention God's name. It is, therefore, not surprising that the Book of Esther was accepted only with difficulty into the canon of Scripture. On the other hand, the obscure origins of the feast should not detract from the artistic and theological values of the book.

Both 3:7 and 9:24 translate "Pur" as "fate." The interpretation is a valid one since the feast focuses on the reversal of the fate of the Jews. Now the vanquished have become the victors and two insignificant Jews have assumed the positions of queen and prime minister. At the same time the word "fate" suggests that Yahweh is somehow involved in the life of his people, although that participation is low key. Hence, while the name of the feast is linked to fate, for the reader it is anything but fate.

Upon reading vv.20-32, the reader senses a certain ennui. The action between the Jewish people and its enemies has been concluded and the appropriate days for the celebration of the victory determined in vv.17-19. Instead of finishing the narrative, the author proceeds to add two more accounts about the celebration of Purim, viz., vv.20-28 and 29-32. One begins to suspect that these verses may not be the work of the author of the narrative. For example, vv.17-18 distinguish between the Jews in the provinces who celebrate on the 14th of Adar and the Jews of Susa who celebrate on the 15th. Verse 19 then links the 14th of Adar celebration with those who live in unwalled cities. However, according to vv.21, 27-28 both the 14th and the 15th of Adar are incumbent on all Jews. Besides, in 9:24 Haman is the one who cast the lot whereas in 3:7 it was someone other than Haman. Apart from 3:7 the casting of the lot has had no impact on the rest of the story until v.26 (see Macc 15:36). How are vv.20-32 related to the rest of the narrative?

Although some scholars consider vv.20-28 the work of a later hand because of the reasons given above, there are also grounds for considering them authentic. Given the key role played by banqueting in the story (and indeed double banquets), one tends to expect the final victory to be linked with a feast and not surprisingly a two-day celebration. Since banquets are the means of empowering and disempowering, it seems only fitting that the empowering of the Jews and the disempowering of their enemies should have a festal setting. Since portions played a key role in 2:9, their prominence in vv.19, 22 is not unexpected. To give gifts is to imitate royal generosity.

Vv.29-32 are more of a problem. In the Purim legislation of vv.17-28 there is no mention of fasting. However, v.31 enjoins fasting and lamenting upon the Jews. Moreover, Esther now appears for the first time since v.13 and indeed at the beginning (v.29) and the end (v.32) of this section. One has the impression that the figure of Esther had to be clarified in the celebration of the feast. Why should Mordecai have to confirm his own law (v.20)? Although fasting is connected with feasting in 4:16; 5:5, it is not unlikely that vv.29-32 are the work of a later editor who wishes to emphasize Esther's importance and so reinstate her position in the feast of Purim.

EPILOGUE
10:1-3.

The author concludes his account by emphasizing the stature of Ahasuerus and Mordecai, his prime minister. The note of peace reminds the reader of all the previous fear and anxiety.

> **10** King Ahasuerus laid tribute on the land and on the coastlands of the sea. ²And all the acts of his power and might, and the full account of the high honor of Mordecai, to which the king advanced him, are they not written in the Book of the Chronicles of the kings of Media and Persia? ³For Mordecai the Jew was next in rank to King Ahasuerus, and he was great among the Jews and popular with the multitude of his brethren, for he sought the welfare of his people and spoke peace to all his people.

The ending is like the beginning but different. The Book of Esther begins and ends with a description of the wealth and power of King Ahasuerus. The splendor of the Persian court and the pageantry of the banquets are echoed in v.2: "and all the acts of power and might." While Ahasuerus' position has remained basically unchanged, Mordecai's position has been radically transformed. With its description of Mordecai's lowly background, 2:6 did not offer the greatest chance for climbing up the bureaucratic ladder. But in vv.2-3 the former exile is more than at home in a foreign country — he is next in rank to the king. The ending here is indeed different.

Presumably the author's mention of tribute on the land and islands (rather than "the coastlands of the sea") seeks to reinforce the power and opulence of the monarch. However, it may also suggest Mordecai's involvement in that wealth. It is at least conceivable that the author is asking his audience to recall Haman's promise of 10,000 talents for the king's treasury (3:9), a promise which involved the demise of the Jewish population. The tribute of v. 1 may imply that the king's wealth is bound up with the perception and statesmanship of his prime minister. Whereas Haman sought his own interests, Mordecai pursued the common good.

What does it mean to be Jewish? The author initiates a dialogue with his audience in raising this question. He has avoided two extremes: (1) concern for the state but without Jewish solidarity; (2) Jewish solidarity but without con-cern for the state. Not surprisingly Mordecai has managed to avoid both extremes. The statement about the king's wealth in v.1 and Mordecai's previous loyalty to the crown (beginning with 2:21-23) dismiss the second extreme. The mention of his popularity and his ongoing efforts to provide for the welfare of his people and to speak peace rule out the first extreme. Mordecai comes off as the very opposite of Haman. Haman sought neither the interests of the crown nor the interests of the Jewish people. Haman took good care of Haman. Mordecai sought both interests. Mordecai took good care of others. The reference to his greatness in v.2 suggests the vast differences in the two prime ministers.

What does it mean to be Jewish? To be Jewish is to look to the needs of fellow Jews. To be Jewish is to identify with their predicament and to undertake a bold course of action, if necessary. In such descriptions the seemingly aloof Yahweh is center stage. The covenant faith of Israel demanded meeting the needs of Yahweh by meeting the needs of Yahweh's people. To serve Yahweh's people is to serve Yahweh. Jewish solidarity entails more than the name "Jewish." It means the willingness to resist oppression and thus promote the welfare and peace of v.3.

However, to be Jewish does not exclude being Persian. The Book of Esther describes Jews who are not on the fringes of Persian politics and society but in the very thick of administration and government. Mordecai is always "Mordecai the Jew" — never "Mordecai the Persian." Yet his politics always envision the good of the Persian state. To those who thought that indifference to the foreign power was the best policy the Book of Esther offers an emphatic no. Allegiance to the God of Israel and the Jewish people does not exclude allegiance to the king of Persia and the Persian people. A Jew is one who provides for other Jews but in so providing envisions a larger arena of human interaction and concern. Mordecai the Jew, the Persian prime minister, symbolizes the tension involved in loyalties but also the happy outcome when the proper balance is achieved.

In reading these final verses, one somehow yearns for a final statement regarding Esther. Like Mordecai, she is a parade example of resolving conflicting loyalties. At the same time she offers a different yet courageous approach in the midst of such loyalties. She combines charm and shrewdness to win over the hesitating Ahasuerus. She is a woman of action, dedicated to the good of her people, yet compelled to accomplish her goals in a way quite different from that of her cousin. If the Jewish audience cheered the achievements of Mordecai, that audience could not entertain less enthusiasm for their beautiful queen.

The call to power has its temptation and its dangers. Esther successfully overcomes them because she sees royal power as power to benefit others (see Ps 72[71]:12-14). (For the opposite see Queen Jezebel in 1 Kgs 21.) Though the Book of Esther is an historical novel, it offers a challenge not always realized in history, viz., the willingness to use power and prestige for others. Esther continues to be a model for ongoing generations of sisters and brothers, although the specific use of power must always be reassessed against the total Word of God.

The Book of Judith

CONTENTS

INTRODUCTION TO
THE BOOK OF JUDITH

The Appeal of the Book

The Book of Judith is the story of one woman pitted against the huge Assyrian war machine. It contrasts the "weak" hand of this woman with the seemingly insuperable might of the greatest commander-in-chief, Holofernes. It is in some ways the female version of David and Goliath. In view of such formidable odds what are the chances for victory and, if one can speak of victory, what are the resources? The author will reply that it is the faith of this woman, a faith which springs from Israel's covenant bond with God.

First of all, the woman herself. While Judith is the embodiment of Israel's covenant faith, she is that embodiment in a typically feminine way. She knows the art of proper make-up and the significance of the right wardrobe. It will be Judith's beauty that will eventually topple the Assyrian forces. She is also the orator. She argues from Israel's history and shows the meaning of resistance. But her presentation is marked by a delicate feminine charm. She is seductive. She knows how to appeal to General Holofernes and entice him, giving the impression that she is the vanquished and he the victor. She knows how to accept the honors of her people and yet keep all possible suitors at a distance. Indeed the author captures her poise and charm by delaying seven chapters before introducing his heroine. (Because of the limitations of space this commentary will deal only with chaps. 8-16.) But the reader feels more than adequately compensated when she arrives in chap. 8 to resolve the problem in a most womanlike manner.

Do you dare to be different? In her opening speech in chap. 8 Judith sees Israel's faith as the willingness to be different from all other nations. Even though all the other nations have capitulated to the Assyrian king and his general, Judith insists that resistance is the only approach consonant with Israel's God. To give up is, in effect, to deny the power of the Lord and his plan for his people. To resist, however, is to acknowledge Israel's proud heritage and Lord's abiding presence. To be a Jew or not to be a Jew — that is the question. It is from Judith (which means "Jewess") that Jews regain the will to live, not merely survive. Judith will be the woman for all seasons, for she is the woman who takes pride in being different and instilling that difference in others.

Take hold of the opportunity. Judith serves as a model for seeing the Assyrian crisis, not merely as a faith crisis, but as a faith opportunity. To believe means to observe the present with discerning eyes and to ask: what can we gain? Judith does not endorse a *deus ex machina*. Her faith demands a middle course. On the one hand, it means rejecting fear. On the other hand, it implies dismissing the dream of heavenly armies which will wipe out the enemy. The faith opportunity is precisely a human opportunity. To seize that opportunity, to approach it with human bravado, and to recognize it as a demonstration of covenant loyalty is not merely to defeat a given enemy but to offer a pattern for future action. Judith is as timely as ever.

Judith is a model of human liberation. As a woman and a widow, she does not enjoy a privileged position in a male-dominated society. Yet, she is the one who boldly suggests the means of countering the Assyrian war machine. She does not manipulate, she does not resort to pious platitudes, she does not hesitate to contradict the male leaders. While she cannot proffer the proof of ultimate victory, she demonstrates how one can be victorious, viz., by thinking in terms of the community.

To effect human liberation is to offer one's whole person and talent for the common good. Human liberation can only be self-fulfilling, if it is self-emptying. The Book of Judith is a dramatic example of one person who thrust aside her personal concerns to address the needs of the larger community. Judith is a model of human liberation because she identifies in terms of the community. She is person for others. The "weak" hand of the woman strikes a mighty blow for Israel's liberation and, at the same time, for human liberation.

Judith challenges the new faith-community. That audience must indeed read Judith, appreciating the author's purpose (see below). But the community must go beyond the author's world to confront the demanding problems of human liberation today. One cannot read Judith in isolation from the Gospel. The community must listen to the entire Word of God and realize that there is no single univocal answer for all times and places. Judith must urge the modern faith-community to understand covenant in a more radical, all-encompassing way. To be Church means to provide for the entire world.

The Setting of the Book

The first seven chapters of the book are not simply a boring catalog of Assyrian successes and non-Assyrian failures. They serve to demonstrate the might of the Assyrians and thus underline the depth of faith required to counteract such might. In so doing, they set the stage for the appearance of Judith in chap. 8.

The story begins with an invitation by the Assyrian king, Nebuchadnezzar, to his vassal states to join in a war against Arphaxad and the Medes in Ecbatana — an invitation which some decline. Once Nebuchadnezzar has defeated the Medes, he turns against those vassals that rejected his invitation. His commander-in-chief, Holofernes, is commissioned to punish these western nations, to wreak havoc and fear, and thus force them to capitulate. Despite great destruction only one nation chooses to hold out — the people of Israel. Realizing the might of the enemy, the Jews plan their strategy and cry to Yahweh for help. When Holofernes learns that only one nation is still insubordinate, Achior, the chief of the Ammonites, explains to him that the Jews enjoy a unique protection from their God, provided they remain faithful to him. Angered by this explanation, Holofernes orders that Achior perish with the Jews.

Achior is left just below Bethulia where the Jewish population of the town rescues him and learns of Nebuchadnezzar's plan to destroy their town and their nation. The Assyrian advance strikes fear in the hearts of the people of Bethulia. When Holofernes cuts off the water supply, the people demand that their leaders surrender the town. Uzziah, the leading authority, accedes to their wish, provided that relief does not come in five days. The concluding words of chap. 7 capture the mood of the people: "And they were greatly depressed in the city" (7:32).

Originally the Jews are simply one nation which sides with the gentile nations to oppose Nebuchadnezzar (1:7-11). Once Nebuchadnezzar moves against these western nations, the Jews and the Gentiles part company. The Gentiles are willing to renounce their gods and swear allegiance to Nebuchadnezzar, while sending their troops to fight with Holofernes (2:28-3:8). Thus, the Jews choose to be different by opposing the Assyrian threat (4:1-13).

The scene moves quickly from Ecbatana to Israel and finally to the town of Bethulia. Bethulia thereby becomes the symbol of resistance to the gigantic coalition of pagan nations. Given the Assyrian success rate, the fall of Bethulia seems imminent. The author demonstrates the impending catastrophe by noting how the Assyrian terror sweeps across the empire. The people along the seacoast experience fear and terror (2:28). Hearing of Holofernes' military successes, the Jews are terrified (4:2). When the Assyrians finally encamp outside Bethulia, "they (the Israelites) were greatly terrified" (7:4). The Jews then cry out to their Lord for help, "for their courage failed" (7:19).

Nebuchadnezzar and Holofernes

In a few quick strokes the author dramatizes the might of Nebuchadnezzar. He mentions the dimensions of the walls of Ecbatana, the Medean city of Arphaxad. The stone blocks of the walls were four and a half feet thick and nine feet long. The walls themselves were 105 feet high and 75 feet thick (1:2). Some verses later the author notes: "he (Nebuchadnezzar) came to Ecbatana, captured its towers, and turned its beauty into shame" (1:14). Who would dare oppose this incredible Assyrian war machine? At the same time Nebuchadnezzar quickly leaves the scene. He has only one first-person speech in 2:5-13. Thereafter his commander-in-chief, Holofernes, commands center stage.

Holofernes (most likely a Persian name) is a study in contrasts. In 6:2 he is the faithful servant who deifies his master: " 'Who is God except Nebuchadnezzar?' " (6:2). Later on, however, he disregards his servant status and chooses to toy with the possibility of becoming a king. He is capricious, lustful, vain. The reader naturally wonders if such weaknesses can perhaps lead to the demise of the world's greatest general. Is it possible that the charm and beauty of a woman may prove to be more challenging than the united strength of the enemy?

Origins and Literary Form

The historical errors in Judith are more glaring than those in Esther. 1:1 identifies Nebuchadnezzar as the Assyrian king who reigned in the city of Nineveh in 593/2 B.C. Actually Nebuchadnezzar was a Babylonian king whose capital was Babylon. Moreover, Nineveh fell seven years before he became king. The passage 1:14 ascribes the conquest of Ecbatana, the capital of the Medes, to Nebuchadnezzar whereas it was only the Persian king, Cyrus, who accomplished this feat in 550 B.C. In 2:21 Holofernes marches his troops in three days from Nineveh to the plain of Bectileth — a distance of some three hundred miles! In 4:6 the author introduces the high priest Joakim who enjoys not only religious but also military authority. However, the combination of such power did not occur until the time of Jonathan, the brother of Judas Maccabeus, in 153 B.C. (see 1 Macc 10:20). Bethulia, the center of resistance, is otherwise unknown.

The historical and geographical blunders may very likely be the author's use of irony. Thus, he may be demonstrating how clever the Jews are and, by the same token, how ignorant pagan readers are. The three-day trek covering three-hundred miles is perhaps another example of such irony. The author gives the impression of titillating and amusing his audience and thereby suggesting that his account will not be sober history.

The history of Israel provides the theological control for assessing the meaning of the book. While seeming to narrate one concrete encounter between a pagan king and Israel, he is actually speaking of an encounter which transcends history and becomes the model of opposition to any and every pagan rule.

Thus, the author invokes the pattern of the Exodus. According to Exod 5:1-2 the contest in Egypt is really between Yahweh and Pharaoh. In Jdt 3:8; 6:2 Nebuchadnezzar is the god who seeks to compel all people to acknowledge him as such. The Book of Judith, therefore, is a confrontation between the divine Nebuchadnezzar and Yahweh, not Nebuchadnezzar/Holofernes and Judith/Israel.

As the Book of Nahum shows, the Assyrians symbolized insolence and rapacity and therefore earned their demise in the late seventh century B.C. Originally Assyria was to be the rod of God's anger against his people (Isa 10:5). However, Assyria exceeded that mandate and provoked Yahweh's condemnation: ". . . and as men gather eggs that have been forsaken so I (Assyria) have gathered all the earth; . . . Therefore the Lord, the Lord of hosts, will send wasting sickness among his stout warriors . . ." (Isa 10:14, 16). In this regard Sennacherib's siege of Jerusalem in 701 B.C. (2 Kgs 18-19; Isa 36-37) is especially significant since it was an attack on Yahweh himself. " 'Who among all the gods of these countries have delivered their countries out of my (Sennacherib's) hand, that the Lord should deliver Jerusalem out of my hand?' " (Isa 36:20). Yahweh's miraculous intervention against Sennacherib in Isa 37:33-37 is a theological precedent for the Book of Judith.

Nebuchadnezzar destroyed Jerusalem in 586 B.C. It was a traumatic experience that Israel never forgot. Nebuchadnezzar thus became the very epitome of opposition, not only to Yahweh's people, but to Yahweh himself. However, as in the case of Assyria, Yahweh inveighed against the tyrant who exceeded the divine mandate: "Sit in silence, and go into darkness, O daughter of the Chaldeans; for you shall no more be called the mistress of kingdoms" (Isa 47:5). Like Pharaoh and Assyria, Babylon found its match in a most worthy opponent — not simply Israel, but Yahweh.

Judith is clearly a rescue story in which the female plays the heroine and saves the male (Israel) from the hand of Holofernes. It is a parade example of resisting the most overwhelming forces. Given the historical errors and the precedents from Israel's history, the book recites history, not in any scientific way, but in a parabolic way. It is the resistance story for every time and place. It is the Exodus story for every generation of Israelites. It would not be far from the mark to label the book a historical novel. Although the book offers evidence of a very concrete situation, it transcends that situation to embrace all situations. Judith is Israel's resistance story par excellence, although it is not necessarily the model of resistance for today's wider audience.

The Author's Purpose

Like Esther, Judith deals with God as the absent hero. For example, only once (4:13) does the narrator make God the subject of a sentence. Unlike Esther, Judith mentions God's name, endorses Jewish practices, refers to the cult in Jerusalem, etc. While the book is the conflict between Nebuchadnezzar and Yahweh, the author necessarily implies human participation. This participation takes the form of allegiance to Yahweh, not to the deified Nebuchadnezzar: " 'But we know no other god but him, and therefore we hope that he will not disdain us or any of our nation' " (8:20). The author is clearly urging his people to a renewed sense of solidarity and coresponsibility. To rally to Judith's proposal is to renew the pledge of allegiance to Yahweh.

What threatened Israel's covenantal faith? It was Hellenism, i.e., the philosophy and way of life introduced by Alexander the Great in 332 B.C. when he swept through Palestine. Unlike the author of the Book of Wisdom, the author of Judith attempts no reconciliation with Hellenistic mores and culture. The Book of Judith reflects the ongoing resistance of the Maccabees to Hellenism, and especially to Antiochus IV Epiphanes (175-164 B.C.) — a resistance captured in First and Second Maccabees. The author encourages his audience to continue this resistance — the cause of the Maccabees should live on in them. As a result, the author promotes a fervent religious-nationalistic mentality, zeal for the Jewish Law, ascetic practices, and concern for the temple in Jerusalem (a contrast with the Book of Esther!). It hardly seems an accident that the heroine's name is the female counterpart of *Judas* Maccabeus. Judith continues to champion Judas' cause.

In providing hope and encouragement for his people, the author writes an account based on Israel's historically founded faith, not simply one episode. The past is invoked to bear on the present in order to offer hope for the future. Israel's history is not a static recitation of long-forgotten events. Israel's history is ever fresh, ever new. By meeting the challenge of the present situation, the Jews prove that they are God's story, that they are the bearers of meaning in their own lives.

Fundamentally Judith is an appeal to identify with a common cause, to find meaning for their lives by accepting the common challenge. As a result, Judith appeals to Christians as well to enflesh their history in the needs of the world-wide community. Evil wears new disguises, manipulation has new masks. Thus understood, Judith announces that the only genuine form of identity derives from contributing one's gifts to this wider community and thereby fulfilling the expectations of a more encompassing covenant faith. The Christian must revive the passion/resurrection story in the debacle of the 20th century. The story of Judith is an ongoing challenge which transcends its own historical and nationalistic parameters. To be moved by Judith is to be led to oppose any and every form of human injustice.

Time of Composition

The Book of Judith was probably written in Hebrew by a Palestinian Jew around 150 B.C. The Hebrew original is no longer extant. However, the Greek text (which exists in three divergent forms) reflects the Hebrew original yet evidences a literary character of its own. (The Greek text uses the Septuagint in a creative way when citing or referring to biblical texts). Like the additions to the Book of Esther, the Book of Judith is a deuterocanonical work. The Greek text is the canonical text. Although the Jewish and Protestant communities do not accept Judith as a book of Scripture, they still recognize its value. Among the Jews Judith is used in the liturgy for the feast of Hanukkah. This feast marks the purification of the temple by Judas Maccabeus and his followers in 164 B.C. Both 8:21 and 9:8 imply the desecration of the temple by the forces of Antiochus IV Epiphanes and lend support to a dating in the mid-second century B.C.

INTRODUCING THE HEROINE
8:1-36

This chapter introduces the heroine to the audience. Within a very short time that audience realizes that Judith is not only beautiful but also competent and anxious for the good of her people. The material may be divided as follows: (1) the background and character of Judith (8:1-10); (2) the speech to the elders and its outcome (8:11-36).

THE BACKGROUND AND CHARACTER OF JUDITH
8:1-10.

8 At that time Judith heard about these things: she was the daughter of Merari the son of Ox, son of Joseph, son of Oziel, son of Elkiah, son of Ananias, son of Gideon, son of Raphaim, son of Ahitub, son of Elijah, son of Hilkiah, son of Eliab, son of Nathanael, son of Salamiel, son of Sarasadai, son of Israel. [2]Her husband Manasseh, who belonged to her tribe and family, had died during the barley harvest. [3]For as he stood overseeing the men who were binding sheaves in the field, he was overcome by the burning heat, and took to his bed and died in Bethulia his city. So they buried him with his fathers in the field between Dothan and Balamon. [4]Judith had lived at home

as a widow for three years and four months. ⁵She set up a
tent for herself on the roof of her house, and girded
sackcloth about her loins and wore the garments of her
widowhood. ⁶She fasted all the days of her widowhood,
except the day before the sabbath and the sabbath itself,
the day before the new moon and the day of the new
moon, and the feasts and days of rejoicing of the house of
Israel. ⁷She was beautiful in appearance, and had a very
lovely face; and her husband Manasseh had left her gold
and silver, and men and women slaves, and cattle, and
fields; and she maintained this estate. ⁸No one spoke ill of
her, for she feared God with great devotion.

⁹When Judith heard the wicked words spoken by the
people against the ruler, because they were faint for lack
of water, and when she heard all that Uzziah said to them,
and how he promised them under oath to surrender the
city to the Assyrians after five days, ¹⁰she sent her maid,
who was in charge of all she possessed, to summon Cha-
bris and Charmis, the elders of her city.

Enter the heroine! The first seven chapters have emphasized the Assyrian might and the Jewish depression. It is at
this point of capitulation that the author introduces the
leading lady. It has been worth the wait. Judith can boast of
purity of descent. Although the genealogy is contrived, it
links "the Jewess" with Israel-Jacob. Indeed, this is the
longest genealogy for any woman in the Bible. By rooting
Judith in the history of Israel, the author is preparing for the
contribution she will make to that ongoing history.

Judith is a widow. The author stresses this point by noting
the circumstances of Manasseh's death and Judith's subsequent mourning. As a widow, she enjoys special protection
from God (see Ps 68 [67]:5; Sir 35:14). As a widow, Judith
symbolizes weakness since she lacks the strength and support of Manasseh. The author will use this weakness/
strength motif to highlight God's modus agendi, viz., weakness overcoming strength. As a widow, Judith dramatizes
the plight of her people: loneliness, rejection, despair. She
is like the guttered Jerusalem: "How lonely sits the city that

was full of people! How like a widow has she become,..."
(Lam 1:1). As a widow and, therefore, a more mature person, Judith provokes less consternation than an unmarried
woman in carrying out her bold plan against Holofernes.

Judith is pious. Unlike Esther, Judith exhibits those practices which mark Jewish piety. She remains faithful to the
memory of her husband by a protracted period of mourning. She erects a tent for herself, so that she can pray
regularly. Like the Maccabean warriors (see 1 Macc 2:14;
3:47), she wears sackcloth and observes the fasts permitted
by the Law. Although she is wealthy, she is generous
towards others (16:18, 23-24).

Judith is beautiful. The author inserts this note between
her fasting and her wealth (v.7). However, he is merely
setting the stage for Judith's bold plan against Holofernes
and the Assyrians since her beauty will serve as a foil. Again
the remark about Judith's mourning is not wasted: just
forty months. Such a period attains two objects. First, it
demonstrates Judith's piety. Secondly, and perhaps more
importantly, it suggests that a longer period would diminish
Judith's beauty and hence make her less of an attraction to
Holofernes.

THE SPEECH TO THE ELDERS
AND ITS OUTCOME
8:11-36.

> [11]They came to her, and she said to them, "Listen to
> me, rulers of the people of Bethulia! What you have said
> to the people today is not right; you have even sworn and
> pronounced this oath between God and you, promising
> to surrender the city to our enemies unless the Lord turns
> and helps us within so many days. [12]Who are you, that
> have put God to the test this day, and are setting your-
> selves up in the place of God among the sons of men?
> [13]You are putting the Lord Almighty to the test—but you
> will never know anything! [14]You cannot plumb the

depths of the human heart, nor find out what a man is thinking; how do you expect to search out God, who made all these things, and find out his mind or comprehend his thought? No, my brethren, do not provoke the Lord our God to anger. [15]For if he does not choose to help us within these five days, he has power to protect us within any time he pleases, or even to destroy us in the presence of our enemies. [16]Do not try to bind the purposes of the Lord our God; for God is not like man, to be threatened, nor like a human being, to be won over by pleading. [17]Therefore, while we wait for his deliverance, let us call upon him to help us, and he will hear our voice, if it pleases him.

[18]"For never in our generation, nor in these present days, has there been any tribe or family or people or city of ours which worshiped gods made with hands, as was done in days gone by—[19]and that was why our fathers were handed over to the sword, and to be plundered, and so they suffered a great catastrophe before our enemies. [20]But we know no other god but him, and therefore we hope that he will not disdain us or any of our nation. [21]For if we are captured all Judea will be captured and our sanctuary will be plundered; and he will exact of us the penalty for its desecration. [22]And the slaughter of our brethren and the captivity of the land and the desolation of our inheritance—all this he will bring upon our heads among the Gentiles, wherever we serve as slaves; and we shall be an offense and a reproach in the eyes of those who acquire us. [23]For our slavery will not bring us into favor, but the Lord our God will turn it to dishonor.

[24]"Now therefore, brethren, let us set an example to our brethren, for their lives depend upon us, and the sanctuary and the temple and the altar rest upon us. [25]In spite of everything let us give thanks to the Lord our God, who is putting us to the test as he did our forefathers. [26]Remember what he did with Abraham, and how he tested Isaac, and what happened to Jacob in Mesopotamia in Syria, while he was keeping the sheep of Laban, his mother's brother. [27]For he has not tried us with fire, as he did them, to search their hearts, nor has he taken revenge upon us; but the Lord scourges those who draw near to him, in order to admonish them."

²⁸Then Uzziah said to her, "All that you have said has been spoken out of a true heart, and there is no one who can deny your words. ²⁹Today is not the first time your wisdom has been shown, but from the beginning of your life all the people have recognized your understanding, for your heart's disposition is right. ³⁰But the people were very thirsty, and they compelled us to do for them what we have promised, and made us take an oath which we cannot break. ³¹So pray for us, since you are a devout woman, and the Lord will send us rain to fill our cisterns and we will no longer be faint."

³²Judith said to them, "Listen to me. I am about to do a thing which will go down through all generations of our descendants. ³³Stand at the city gate tonight, and I will go out with my maid; and within the days after which you have promised to surrender the city to our enemies, the Lord will deliver Israel by my hand. ³⁴Only, do not try to find out what I plan; for I will not tell you until I have finished what I am about to do."

³⁵Uzziah and the rulers said to her, "Go in peace, and may the Lord God go before you, to take revenge upon our enemies." ³⁶So they returned from the tent and went to their posts.

Judith is courageous. In a male-dominated society it is Judith who summons the elders and takes them to task. In vv.28-31 Mayor Uzziah comes off as less than courageous: "'But the people were very thirsty, and they compelled us...'" (v.30). On the other hand, Judith lives up to her name — she is the embodiment of the true Israel. Nothing less than the honor of the country is at stake (vv.21-23). In her logic the situation calls for calculated risks. Moreover, such action will set an example for the rest of the people (v.24). Her courage moves her to think in terms of others, viz., the people of Isreal together with their temple and sanctuary. The woman's hand (v.33) is anything but weak.

Judith is wise. She reflects the wisdom of the woman of Abel of Beth-maacah who recommended the execution of Sheba in order to preserve the common good (see 2 Sam 20:14-22). Judith argues that one cannot set up parameters for God. The five-day limit means tempting God (v.12-13). She thereby strikes a blow for God's liberty — she allows God to be God, not a puppet to be cajoled and manipulated by human imperatives (vv.15-16).

Judith also rejects the suggestion that God is punishing the people since according to v.20 they are righteous. Her wisdom betrays Israel's covenant faith (v.20). However, to surrender to Holofernes is to acknowledge Nebuchadnezzar as god (6:2). Judith concludes that the present impasse is really a trial. God is testing them as he tested their ancestors (v.26). After the manner of the wisdom literature (see Job 5:17-18; Prov 3:12) Judith urges that such testing goes hand in hand with God's loving concern. After such a display the reader is not surprised by Uzziah's comment: " 'Today is not the first time your wisdom has been shown, . . . ' " (v.29). Ironically, the foolish woman has outwitted the wise old man.

The author suggests a link with Israel's Exodus experience. The Greek verb in the phrase " 'The Lord will deliver Israel' " (v.33) reflects Yahweh's concern for his people in Egypt (Exod 3:16) and his care for them as demonstrated in his providing for the patriarch Joseph (Exod 13:19). The instrument for effecting this deliverance will be Judith's hand (v.33) — a motif to which the author will return several times, implying a connection with God's hand now and Moses' hand in the first Exodus.

Regarding Bethulia (which probably means "House of God") the question is not: where is Bethulia? but rather: what is Bethulia? According to the book Bethulia is located in Samaria, opposite Esdraelon in the Plain of Dothan (4:6). It is on a hilltop above the valley (10:10), flanked by mountains (6:10-12) and close to springs (6:11). However, no one has ever succeeded in discovering Bethulia. The author is more interested in the meaning of Bethulia, not its location. Bethulia is really Jerusalem. In 8:24 the fate of the sanctuary is in the hands of the elders. In 9:8, 13 Judith prays for reprisals against those who plan to desecrate Zion and its sanctuary. In their farewell greeting (10:8) the elders connect Judith's exploits with the exaltation of Jerusalem (see also 13:4). In 15:9 Judith is hailed as the exaltation of Jerusalem.

Judith, therefore, is not simply an individual — she is also a corporate personality. She represents the best of Israel and thus attempts to have the elders emulate her. "The Jewess" identifies with the very heart of Judaism, Jerusalem. Because of her daring, cunning, and faith Bethulia, i.e., Jerusalem, will be safe. Such an identification, moreover, fits in with the suggested time of composition, i.e., the mid-second century B.C. following the exploits of the Maccabeans to wrest Jerusalem and its temple from the Hellenists.

The author deftly handles suspense, interest, and curiosity. Besides tempting God (vv.12, 15), the five-day limit arouses the reader's curiosity. Since the mayor is bound by an oath, will Judith be able to accomplish her exploit within the allotted time? The author piques the reader's interest when he mentions " 'a thing which will go down through all generations' " (v.32). What thing? Verse 34 involves the reader's ignorance as well. Judith warns the elders not to find out her plan. The reader begins to suspect that the Lord has already acted in her favor and hence the exultation of the later chapters can actually begin now.

JUDITH'S PRAYER
9:1-14

Having resolved to aid her people, Judith calls upon the Lord in prayer. Her prayer is the only fitting preparation for her action against Holofernes and the Assyrians.

9 Then Judith fell upon her face, and put ashes on her head, and uncovered the sackcloth she was wearing; and at the very time when that evening's incense was being offered in the house of God in Jerusalem, Judith cried out to the Lord with a loud voice, and said,

²"O Lord God of my father Simeon, to whom thou gavest a sword to take revenge on the strangers who had loosed the girdle of a virgin to defile her, and uncovered her thigh to put her to shame, and polluted her womb to disgrace her; for thou hast said, 'It shall not be done'—yet they did it. ³So thou gavest up their rulers to be slain, and their bed, which was ashamed of the deceit they had practiced, to be stained with blood, and thou didst strike down slaves along with princes, and princes on their thrones; ⁴and thou gavest their wives for a prey and their daughters to captivity, and all their booty to be divided among thy beloved sons, who were zealous for thee, and abhorred the pollution of their blood, and called on thee for help—O God, my God, hear me also, a widow.

⁵"For thou hast done these things and those that went before and those that followed; thou hast designed the

things that are now, and those that are to come. Yea, the things thou didst intend came to pass, ⁶and the things thou didst presented themselves and said, 'Lo, we are here'; for all thy ways are prepared in advance, and thy judgment is with foreknowledge.

⁷"Behold now, the Assyrians are increased in their might; they are exalted, with their horses and riders; they glory in the strength of their foot soldiers; they trust in shield and spear, in bow and sling, and know not that thou art the Lord who crushest wars; the Lord is thy name. ⁸Break their strength by thy might, and bring down their power in thy anger; for they intend to defile thy sanctuary, and to pollute the tabernacle where thy glorious name rests, and to cast down the horn of thy altar with the sword. ⁹Behold their pride, and send thy wrath upon their heads; give to me, a widow, the strength to do what I plan. ¹⁰By the deceit of my lips strike down the slave with the prince and the prince with his servant; crush their arrogance by the hand of a woman.

¹¹"For thy power depends not upon numbers, nor thy might upon men of strength; for thou art God of the lowly, helper of the oppressed, upholder of the weak, protector of the forlorn, savior of those without hope. ¹²Hear, O hear me, God of my father, God of the inheritance of Israel, Lord of heaven and earth, Creator of the waters, King of all thy creation, hear my prayer! ¹³Make my deceitful words to be their wound and stripe, for they have planned cruel things against thy covenant, and against thy consecrated house, and against the top of Zion, and against the house possessed by thy children. ¹⁴And cause thy whole nation and every tribe to know and understand that thou art God, the God of all power and might, and that there is no other who protects the people of Israel but thou alone!"

Judith's piety is evident again. Uncovering her sackcloth (worn under the outer garments), Judith culminates the prayer of lamentation begun by the people in 4:9-15 (see also 6:18-19; 7:19). A communal lament (Judith prays for herself only as God's instrument) presupposes that Israel's problem has become God's problem and that God's problem has become Israel's   problem. The plight of Bethulia thus becomes God's problem and Judith's role in that plight is now Israel's problem. The prayer assumes that the Lord is still interested in and bound up with Israel's destiny. For Judith God is still in charge — nothing escapes his attention and nothing surpasses his strength (vv.5-6).

Judith sees continuity in the faith history of Israel. She appeals to Simeon's deed and employs it as a precedent for God's action now against the Assyrians. Verses 2, 4 refer to Gen 34, i.e., Simeon's act of revenge (together with his brother Levi) on the Shechemites for Shechem's rape of their sister Dinah. Although Gen 49:5 criticizes their action, Judith interprets it in terms of national honor and solidarity. Just as Shechem defiled Dinah and polluted her womb (v.2), the Assyrians now seek to defile the sanctuary and pollute the tabernacle (v.8). Shechem raped a virgin, Assyria now threatens a widow, Israel/Judith.

Israel's existence is at stake. The author seems to evoke the image of Israel as Yahweh's bride but a bride who is in danger of being defiled (see Jer 3:1-2; Ezek 16, 23; Hos 2:9-10). The words "sword" (v.2) and "bed" (v.3) foreshadow 13:1-9 where Judith will use a sword to slay Holofernes as he lies in a drunken stupor in his bed. The possible defilement of Judith symbolizes the danger of Israel. Judith's honor and Israel's honor are interwoven. However, Judith's integrity (see 8:8) suggests that Israel will maintain her integrity (see 16:22).

Judith's deed will be the Exodus revisited. In Simeon's retaliation God struck down " 'slaves along with princes, and princes on their thrones' " (v.3; see v.10). This is precisely God's action in the Exodus when he strikes down the first-born, even the first-born of Pharaoh who sits upon his throne (see Exod 11:5; 12:29). " 'The Lord who crushest wars; the Lord is thy name' " (v.7) is the Greek text of Exod 15:3, the song which celebrates Yahweh's defeat of Pharaoh and the Egyptians at the Reed Sea. The sending of wrath on the Assyrians echoes Yahweh's action in the same song (see Exod 15:7). When the very life of God's people is at stake,

Judith uses phrases which capture God's action at the very beginning of his people in Egypt. Yahweh who confronted and defeated Pharaoh can thus confront and defeat the new Pharaoh, the divine Nebuchadnezzar in the person of his general.

The hand motif, hinted at in 8:33, is now exploited and linked with the new Exodus. Verse 2 reads literally:" 'my father Simeon into whose *hand* you gave a sword.' " Verse 9 also reads literally: " 'give to my hand — the widow's — the strength.' " Verse 10 concludes: " 'Crush their arrogance by the hand of a woman.' " The precedent here is Yahweh's action in the Exodus: " 'thy right hand, O Lord, shatters the enemy' " (Exod 15:6). Significantly Exod 15:9 puts these words on the lips of Yahweh's enemies: " 'I will draw my sword, my *hand* shall destroy them.' " Judith, therefore, prays that her hand will shatter the Assyrians as God's hand shattered the Egyptians. In Judith's deed the Exodus lives on.

The chapter suggests Judith's course of action against Holofernes, viz., a sword wielded by the "weak" hand of a woman. It also implies the humiliation which will befall Holofernes. To be killed by a woman is the greatest insult. Thus, in Judg 9:54 Abimelech tells his armor-bearer: " 'Draw your sword and kill me, lest men say of me, "A woman killed him." ' "

In vv.10, 13 Judith speaks of the deceit, the ruse she will employ against the enemy. Again the author arouses the curiosity of his audience, making them all the more anxious to know what the clever woman is devising against the world's greatest general. Although such deceit causes moral difficulties for some, the author probably understands Judith's deceit within the framework of the national crisis. Although he does not endorse a program of "all's fair in love and war," he measures Judith's tactics against the common good, and indeed in a situation which involves love and war.

The weakness/strength motif appears in Judith's prayer. Verse 7 captures the Assyrian source of strength: horses, riders, shield, spear, etc. In the following verse the author contrasts such a display of power with Yahweh's awesome might: " 'Break their strength by thy might, and bring down their power in thy anger.' " According to v.11 the Lord does not need arsenals replete with the latest weapons. Paradoxically, Yahweh demonstrates his might in weakness, for he is the " 'God of the lowly, helper of the oppressed, upholder of the weak' " (v.11). It is only a situation of powerlessness that will show Yahweh's true power and concern for his people. Only in this way will all the world acknowledge, not Nebuchadnezzar, but the God of Israel. Yahweh rejects an arms race and replaces such tactics with: " 'The bows of the mighty are broken, but the feeble gird on strength' " (1 Sam 2:4; see Jdt 16:11-12).

JUDITH'S DEPARTURE AND ARRIVAL 10:1-23.

Judith prepares for her encounter with Holofernes. Her departure and arrival are calculated to initiate the process of victory for Israel. The material may be divided as follows: (1) the beauty process (10:1-5); (2) the beauty pageant (10:6-23).

THE BEAUTY PROCESS
10:1-5.

10 When Judith had ceased crying out to the God of Israel, and had ended all these words, ²she rose from where she lay prostrate and called her maid and went down into the house where she lived on sabbaths and on her feast days; ³and she removed the sackcloth which she had been wearing, and took off her widow's garments, and bathed her body with water, and anointed herself with precious ointment, and combed her hair and put on a tiara, and arrayed herself in her gayest apparel, which she used to wear while her husband Manasseh was living. ⁴And she put sandals on her feet, and put on her anklets and bracelets and rings, and her earrings and all her ornaments, and made herself very beautiful, to entice the eyes of all men who might see her. ⁵And she gave her maid

a bottle of wine and a flask of oil, and filled a bag with
parched grain and a cake of dried fruit and fine bread;
and she wrapped up all her vessels and gave them to her to
carry.

Why such a delay? The reader already knows that with the
five-day limit time is running out for the inhabitants of
Bethulia. After her prayer for strength and the inter-play of
"hand" and "sword" one might expect the heroine to conceal a weapon or at least map out some form of military
strategy. She appears to do precisely the opposite. The
action now moves from the prayer room to the beauty
parlor. The scene includes undressing, a beauty bath, perfumes, hair styling, a new hat, a dress from her married days
(see 16:8), attractive footwear (see 16:9), and jewelry for her
ankles, arms, fingers, and ears. There is something of an
understatement when the author comments: "and made
herself very beautiful . . ." (v.4). The reader has reason to ask
how the cosmetics and the beauty treatment are related to
the siege of Bethulia.

The change of apparel and outward appearance is a
change of destiny. Judith recalls the renewed Jerusalem:
"Awake, awake, . . . put on your beautiful garments . . .
Shake yourself from the dust, arise, O captive Jerusalem. . . " (Isa 52:1-2; see also Bar 5:1-2). Judith's regained
beauty symbolizes Israel's deliverance: the end of the siege
and the preparations for celebration. As in Second Isaiah,
we have a transformation leading from death to life. In
putting aside her widow's garb, Judith begins that course of
action which will culminate in a new life for her people and,
ironically, a life brought about by Holofernes' death.

The beauty process disguises Judith as a female warrior.
Actually she has mapped out a military strategy and con-
cealed a weapon. Her beauty is that strategy and weapon.
The female sets out to rescue the male (Israel) and uses that
weapon which she knows will result in victory. This military
approach combines her wisdom with beauty. Judith per-
ceives that her ravishing beauty is the most effective

weapon to win the day. In the person of Judith a female warrior prepares to invade the camp of the world's greatest male warrior. Instead of the usual military hardware she enters the combat zone with the armor of jewelry and the battle plan of seduction.

The Old Testament certainly provides prototypes for Judith the female warrior. In Judg 4-5 it is Deborah ("bee") who demonstrates more initiative than Barak ("lightning") in routing the Canaanite general, Sisera. In these same chapters it is Jael, the wife of Heber, who kills Sisera by driving a peg into his temple while he sleeps. The weakness/strength motif returns. Ironically, it is women like the "bee" who prove to be more resourceful than men like the "lightning" and thereby win victory for the people of Israel.

Provisions are also in order. In 2:17-18 Holofernes collects huge amounts of provisions for his forces. In v.5 Judith takes provisions for herself and her maid for their stay in the Assyrian camp. Judith's provisions clearly indicate that she observes the dietary prescriptions. Thus, she will not become ritually unclean by eating non-kosher food. At the same time Judith makes provisions for other uses of the food bag. The passage 13:9 attests that the bag was also intended for large game!

THE BEAUTY PAGEANT
10:6-23.

> 6Then they went out to the city gate of Bethulia, and found Uzziah standing there with the elders of the city, Chabris and Charmis. 7When they saw her, and noted how her face was altered and her clothing changed, they greatly admired her beauty, and said to her, 8"May the God of our fathers grant you favor and fulfil your plans, that the people of Israel may glory and Jerusalem may be exalted." And she worshiped God.
> 9Then she said to them, "Order the gate of the city to be opened for me, and I will go out and accomplish the

things about which you spoke with me." So they ordered the young men to open the gate for her, as she had said. [10]When they had done this, Judith went out, she and her maid with her; and the men of the city watched her until she had gone down the mountain and passed through the valley and they could no longer see her.

[11]The women went straight on through the valley; and an Assyrian patrol met her [12]and took her into custody, and asked her, "To what people do you belong, and where are you coming from, and where are you going?" She replied, "I am a daughter of the Hebrews, but I am fleeing from them, for they are about to be handed over to you to be devoured. [13]I am on my way to the presence of Holofernes the commander of your army, to give him a true report; and I will show him a way by which he can go and capture all the hill country without losing one of his men, captured or slain."

[14]When the men heard her words, and observed her face—she was in their eyes marvelously beautiful—they said to her, [15]"You have saved your life by hurrying down to the presence of our lord. Go at once to his tent; some of us will escort you and hand you over to him. [16]And when you stand before him, do not be afraid in your heart, but tell him just what you have said, and he will treat you well."

[17]They chose from their number a hundred men to accompany her and her maid, and they brought them to the tent of Holofernes. [18]There was great excitement in the whole camp, for her arrival was reported from tent to tent, and they came and stood around her as she waited outside the tent of Holofernes while they told him about her. [19]And they marveled at her beauty, and admired the Israelites, judging them by her, and every one said to his neighbor, "Who can despise these people, who have women like this among them? Surely not a man of them had better be left alive, for if we let them go they will be able to ensnare the whole world!"

[20]Then Holofernes' companions and all his servants came out and led her into the tent. [21]Holofernes was resting on his bed, under a canopy which was woven with purple and gold and emeralds and precious stones.

²²When they told him of her he came forward to the front of the tent, with silver lamps carried before him. ²³And when Judith came into the presence of Holofernes and his servants, they all marveled at the beauty of her face; and she prostrated herself and made obeisance to him, and his slaves raised her up.

The trek from Bethulia to the Assyrian camp is a beauty pageant. In v.4 the author cautioned his audience that Judith's rediscovered beauty was "to entice the eyes of all men who might see her." In v.7 Uzziah and the two elders take due note of Judith's stunning appearance. If she was already reputed to be a beauty in 8:8, how much more attractive is she now and what effect will she have on the enemy? In v.14 the Assyrian sentries are bewitched by her beauty and in v.17 provide a bodyguard of no less than one hundred soldiers to escort her to Holofernes' tent. Her arrival causes great excitement, so much so that the soldiers abandon their military discipline to cast their eyes on the ravishing Jewish beauty (vv.18-19). Finally in v.23 Holofernes and his servants marvel at her great beauty. The beauty of one woman has upset the organization of the world's greatest army. It is likely, therefore, that Judith's "weapon" will succeed.

The journey highlights the courage and boldness of Judith and her maid. They leave the relative security of Bethulia to make their way into the dangers of an enemy camp. Their plan is somehow to win the cooperation of the enemy and thus reach the commander. The bold plan works. In this one short journey they have won the good will of the Assyrians and Judith has captured the heart of their general.

Sexual imagery explains Judith's military strategy against Holofernes. According to 4:7 the entrance to the city of Bethulia is narrow. Holofernes' plan is to penetrate the city; Judith's strategy is to prevent him from penetrating. The heroine has to use her sexual appeal to destroy the enemy but without allowing herself to be used by Holo-

fernes in the process. In the final scene the general tries to
penetrate but is beheaded in the process.

There is a touch of irony in the sentries' remark to Judith
that she has saved her life by hastening to meet Holofernes
(v.14). In the end Judith's arrival at Holofernes' tent will
cost him his life. In v.19 the Jewish women are the pride of
the nation, yet the Assyrians dare not allow a Jewish man to
live, lest the Jews gain the upper hand in the world. Ironically, it will be the "Jewess" par excellence who will prevent
the Assyrians from gaining the upper hand in Bethulia.

THE FIRST CONVERSATION BETWEEN JUDITH AND HOLOFERNES
11:1-23

The author now narrates the first dialog between Judith and Holofernes. In so doing he reveals the strengths of Judith and the weaknesses of Holofernes. The material may be divided as follows: (1) Holofernes' welcoming remarks (11:1-4); (2) Judith's speech to Holofernes (11:5-19); (3) the reactions to the speech (11:20-23).

HOLOFERNES' WELCOMING REMARKS
11:1-4.

> **11** Then Holofernes said to her, "Take courage, woman, and do not be afraid in your heart, for I have never hurt any one who chose to serve Nebuchadnezzar, the king of all the earth. ²And even now, if your people who live in the hill country had not slighted me, I would never have lifted my spear against them; but they have brought all this on themselves. ³And now tell me why you have fled from them and have come over to us—since you have come to safety. ⁴Have courage; you will live, tonight and from now on. No one will hurt you, but all will treat you well, as they do the servants of my lord King Nebuchadnezzar."

In his first conversation with Judith Holofernes' sensuality and vanity command attention. In 10:23 the author remarked that Judith's beauty had captivated the mighty general. (See his expression of admiration in vv.21, 23.) In these opening verses his vanity is evident. His welcoming address is not unlike the oracles of salvation in Second Isaiah. For example, "'Fear not, for I have redeemed you;... For I am,...your Savior...you are precious in my eyes, and honoured, and I love you...'" (Isa 43:1,3,4). It should not noted that Judith does not hesitate to support his vanity (see v.7 and compare with Dan 2:38).

JUDITH'S SPEECH TO HOLOFERNES
11:5-19.

⁵Judith replied to him, "Accept the words of your servant, and let your maidservant speak in your presence, and I will tell nothing false to my lord this night. ⁶And if you follow out the words of your maidservant, God will accomplish something through you, and my lord will not fail to achieve his purposes. ⁷Nebuchadnezzar the king of the whole earth lives, and as his power endures, who has sent you to direct every living soul, not only do men serve him because of you, but also the beasts of the field and the cattle and the birds of the air will live by your power under Nebuchadnezzar and all his house. ⁸For we have heard of your wisdom and skill, and it is reported throughout the whole world that you are the one good man in the whole kingdom, thoroughly informed and marvelous in military strategy.

⁹"Now as for the things Achior said in your council, we have heard his words, for the men of Bethulia spared him and he told them all he had said to you. ¹⁰Therefore, my lord and master, do not disregard what he said, but keep it in your mind, for it is true: our nation cannot be punished, nor can the sword prevail against them, unless they sin against their God.

¹¹"And now, in order that my lord may not be defeated and his purpose frustrated, death will fall upon them, for a sin has overtaken them by which they are about to

provoke their God to anger when they do what is wrong. [12]Since their food supply is exhausted and their water has almost given out, they have planned to kill their cattle and have determined to use all that God by his laws has forbidden them to eat. [13]They have decided to consume the first fruits of the grain and the tithes of the wine and oil, which they had consecrated and set aside for the priests who minister in the presence of our God at Jerusalem—although it is not lawful for any of the people so much as to touch these things with their hands. [14]They have sent men to Jerusalem, because even the people living there have been doing this, to bring back to them permission from the senate. [15]When the word reaches them and they proceed to do this, on that very day they will be handed over to you to be destroyed.

[16]"Therefore, when I, your servant, learned all this, I fled from them; and God has sent me to accomplish with you things that will astonish the whole world, as many as shall hear about them. [17]For your servant is religious, and serves the God of heaven day and night; therefore, my lord, I will remain with you, and every night your servant will go out into the valley, and I will pray to God and he will tell me when they have committed their sins. [18]And I will come and tell you, and then you shall go out with your whole army, and not one of them will withstand you. [19]Then I will lead you through the middle of Judea, till you come to Jerusalem; and I will set your throne in the midst of it; and you will lead them like sheep that have no shepherd, and not a dog will so much as open its mouth to growl at you. For this has been told me, by my foreknowledge; it was announced to me, and I was sent to tell you."

In order to be successful, Judith's strategy must accomplish certain goals. First, she must win over the general and thereby gain his trust. The opening and closing verses show that Judith has succeeded admirably. Second, she must prevent an immediate Assyrian attack since the enemy would easily defeat the Jews. Her ploy is delay. Hence she insists upon the need for a divine oracle, assuring her of her people's sin (vv.17-18). Third, she must be alone with the general at his most vulnerable moment. The banquet in chap. 12 will provide such an opportunity. Fourth, she must have an escape route which will arouse no suspicion and thus enable her to communicate the demise of Holofernes to the Jews. Her proposal to spend the nights in the valley (v.18) assures such an escape route. The disguised female warrior is a most cunning adversary.

Judith articulates her challenge to Holofernes in the subtle words of v.11: " '. . . that my lord may not be defeated and his purpose frustrated, . . .' " Her whole mission is to penetrate the weakness of the general in order to defeat him and frustrate his purpose. The challenged has now become the challenger, the timid one is already an object of fear. In this challenge Judith will succeed where Achior, the leader of the Ammonites, failed. In 5:5-21 Achior (probably Ahiqar, the sage at the court of Sennacherib — see the Book of Tobit) had explained to Holofernes that only violation of covenant would bring about the defeat of Israel. Like Judith, he promised in 5:5: " 'No falsehood shall come from your servant's mouth.' " Unlike Judith, he did not convince Holofernes and was condemned to perish with the Jews in Bethulia. The foolish woman has defeated the wise man. Our author suggests that her challenge will ultimately win the day.

In order to accomplish her task, Judith must now hold forth on priestly matters. Although women could not join the ranks of the priests, Judith appears as one totally conversant with the distinctions between the sacred and the profane. The food supply as well as the water supply is depleted. As a result, the population has decided to violate their law by eating those parts of the cattle reserved to God and the priests. Similarly they are also seeking permission to eat the first fruits and tithes, although these are reserved by law to the priests and the Levites. While the author certainly underlines the shrewdness of Judith's plan, he may also be reminding his audience of the value of Jewish dietary legislation in view of the inroads of Hellenism (see Dan 1:15-16).

Double meanings are not lacking. In v.6 God will indeed accomplish "something" through Holofernes. But Judith and Holofernes take "something" in completely different senses. In the second half of v.6 "my lord" may mean either Holofernes or the Lord. In v.16 the things that will truly astonish the whole world mean the capture of both Bethulia and Judith for Holofernes, but the lifting of the siege and the death of Holofernes for Judith. In v.19 Judith promises to lead Holofernes to a throne in Jerusalem where Holofernes will then lead the Jews " 'like sheep that have no shepherd.' " According to Num 27:17; 1 Kgs 22:17 the expression means "leaderless" whereas for Holofernes it means an easy victory.

There may also be allusions to the Exodus experience. According to Exod 5:1-2 the Exodus is really a contest between Yahweh and Pharaoh. In the Book of Judith the contest is now between Yahweh and Nebuchadnezzar, the new Pharaoh. Verse 7 describes Nebuchadnezzar (see also v.1) as " 'the king of the whole earth.' " In 6:2 Holofernes raises the question: " 'Who is God except Nebuchadnezzar?' " In the Book of Exodus Moses exacts gradual recognition from Pharaoh with regard to Yahweh. In Exod 8:10 Pharaoh learns that Yahweh has no equal and in 8:22 that Yahweh is in the midst of Egypt. In Exod 9:14 Pharaoh must admit that there is none like Yahweh in all the earth and in Exod 9:29 that the earth belongs to Yahweh. The author of Judith may be implying that Pharaoh's confession will apply to the Assyrians as well, that Judith's hand, like Moses' hand, will force the pagans to acknowledge that Yahweh still defeats modern forms of Pharaoh.

THE REACTIONS TO THE SPEECH
11:20-23.

> [20]Her words pleased Holofernes and all his servants, and they marveled at her wisdom and said, [21]"There is not such a woman from one end of the earth to the other,

either for beauty of face or wisdom of speech!" ²²And Holofernes said to her, "God has done well to send you before the people, to lend strength to our hands and to bring destruction upon those who have slighted my lord. ²³You are not only beautiful in appearance, but wise in speech; and if you do as you have said, your God shall be my God, and you shall live in the house of King Nebuchadnezzar and be renowned throughout the whole world.

Judith is not only a king-maker but also a convert-maker. In v.19 she offered a throne to Holofernes, provided he would accede to her strategy. (One wonders, therefore, if Holofernes is paying only lip service to his lord Nebuchadnezzar and is actually more vain than originally thought.) In this section Judith wins a convert, since Holofernes replies in v.23 that Judith's God will be his God. Although pagans could easily accept the gods of another people or locale, the author may yet be intimating that Judith has succeeded where Achior had failed. Holofernes has accepted Judith's version of Yahweh, not Achior's. The bewitching beauty of Bethulia has "sold" her God to the Assyrians but the sale will demand an awesome price.

JUDITH'S STRATEGY
12:1-20.

The author quickly reveals Judith's strategy. Her eating and praying are part of her plan against Holofernes. She waits until the banquet provides the right moment to execute her plan. The material may be divided as follows: (1) Judith's food and prayer (12:1-9); (2) the banquet and its effect (12:10-20).

JUDITH'S FOOD AND PRAYER
12:1-9.

12 Then he commanded them to bring her in where his silver dishes were kept, and ordered them to set a table for her with some of his own food and to serve her with his own wine. ²But Judith said, "I cannot eat it, lest it be an offense; but I will be provided from the things I have brought with me." ³Holofernes said to her, "If your supply runs out, where can we get more like it for you? For none of your people is here with us." ⁴Judith replied, "As your soul lives, my lord, your servant will not use up the things I have with me before the Lord carries out by my hand what he has determined to do."

⁵Then the servants of Holofernes brought her into the tent, and she slept until midnight. Along toward the

morning watch she arose ⁶and sent to Holofernes and said, "Let my lord now command that your servant be permitted to go out and pray." ⁷So Holofernes commanded his guards not to hinder her. And she remained in the camp for three days, and went out each night to the valley of Bethulia, and bathed at the spring in the camp. ⁸When she came up from the spring she prayed the Lord God of Israel to direct her way for the raising up of her people. ⁹So she returned clean and stayed in the tent until she ate her food toward evening.

The irony continues. In v.4 Judith reassures Holofernes that her kosher food supply will last until she accomplishes the Lord's plan. Her answer is prompted by Holofernes' observation that there are no Jews in the Assyrian camp to provide such food (v.3). However, before the food runs out, there will be a superabundance of Jews in the camp.

Three days of resistance. Judith's preoccupation with dietary laws (vv.1-4; see also v.19) and ritual ablutions (vv.7-9) is not divorced from her image as the pious Jewess. However, the author may be suggesting another image, viz., resistance to sexual violation. Earlier (2:21) Holofernes marched his troops for *three* days prior to ravaging and plundering the enemies of his lord. According to v.7 Judith has remained *three* days in the camp and on the fourth day receives Holofernes' invitation (v.10). Unlike the ravaged nations, Judith has been able to keep her opponent at bay. Her ruse may be that she is menstruating and hence must bathe in the spring at night (v.9: "So she returned clean...."). Such a ruse gains time for executing her plan. Holofernes is becoming more sexually aroused and therefore more vulnerable. The reader wonders if the pure waters of the spring will restrain the passionate consumption of wine (v.20).

Judith's hand is significant in this chapter as well. In v.4 she speaks of what the Lord will carry out by her hand. Judith's revenge on the Assyrians is like Nebuchadnezzar's revenge on the insubordinate nations in 2:12 where his hand will execute what his mouth has spoken. Both texts suggest use of Isa 14:24-27:   " 'and as I have purposed, so shall it stand, that I will break the Assyrian in my land ... this is the *hand* that is stretched out over all the nations . . . His (Yahweh's) *hand* is stretched out, and who will turn it back?'" In Bethulia the Lord will use the hand of Judith to execute his plan. In this way Judith's hand "'will break the Assyrian in my land.'"

The Exodus connection returns in v.5, not in connection with Yahweh's hand (Exod 15:6), but in connection with "the morning watch." It was in the morning watch that the Lord attacked the Egyptians and clogged their chariot wheels — an event which forces the Egyptians to acknowledge that the Lord fought for Israel against the Egyptians (see Exod 14:24-25). It was also toward morning that the Reed Sea resumed its normal depth (Exod 14:27). Judith sleeps until midnight (v.5) — the very time when the Lord slaughtered the first-born.

THE BANQUET AND ITS EFFECT
12:10-20.

¹⁰On the fourth day Holofernes held a banquet for his slaves only, and did not invite any of his officers. ¹¹And he said to Bagoas, the eunuch who had charge of all his personal affairs, "Go now and persuade the Hebrew woman who is in your care to join us and eat and drink with us. ¹²For it will be a disgrace if we let such a woman go without enjoying her company, for if we do not embrace her she will laugh at us." ¹³So Bagoas went out from the presence of Holofernes, and approached her and said, "This beautiful maidservant will please come to my lord and be honored in his presence, and drink wine and be merry with us, and become today like one of the daughters of the Assyrians who serve in the house of Nebuchadnezzar." ¹⁴And Judith said, "Who am I, to refuse my lord? Surely whatever pleases him I will do at once, and it will be a joy to me until the day of my death!" ¹⁵So she got up and arrayed herself in all her woman's finery, and her maid went and spread on the ground for her before Holofernes the soft fleeces which she had

received from Bagoas for her daily use, so that she might recline on them when she ate.

[16]Then Judith came in and lay down, and Holofernes' heart was ravished with her and he was moved with great desire to possess her; for he had been waiting for an opportunity to deceive her, ever since the day he first saw her. [17]So Holofernes said to her, "Drink now, and be merry with us!" [18]Judith said, "I will drink now, my lord, because my life means more to me today than in all the days since I was born." [19]Then she took and ate and drank before him what her maid had prepared. [20]And Holofernes was greatly pleased with her and drank a great quantity of wine, much more than he had ever drunk in any one day since he was born.

Banquets are not unusual in the Book of Judith. In 1:16 Nebuchadnezzar ate and drank for one hundred and twenty days after the death of Arphaxad and the fall of Ecbatana. The banquet of v.10 should be a victory celebration of sorts for Holofernes, viz., his conquest of Judith. In 6:21 Uzziah treated Achior and the elders to a banquet but the joy of celebration was intermingled with cries for help. The banquet of chap. 12 is calculated to silence the Jewish cries for help and cede to their prolonged celebration, i.e., all the way from Bethulia to Jerusalem (see 16:20).

As in the Book of Esther, this banquet looks to empowering/disempowering. Just as the banquets in Esther led to the demise of Vashti and Haman, so too the banquet in Judith will lead to the demise of Holofernes and the Assyrians. In turn, Judith/Israel will share the exultation of Esther and Mordecai. The banquet captures the life/death motif. It will mean life for Judith/Israel but death for Holofernes/Assyria.

A sexual atmosphere pervades this section. In v.15 Judith the warrior resorts to her sexual arsenal. In putting on her party dress and in adorning herself, the heroine prepares to take advantage of the sexually vulnerable Holofernes. The author heightens the sexual atmosphere by mentioning the soft fleeces which serve for reclining while she eats. The combination of food, furniture, and violation is reminiscent of the scene in 2 Sam 13:7-14 where Tamar, Absalom's sister, brings food to her half-brother Amnon as he lies in bed pretending to be sick. Amnon's violation of Tamar is consonant with Holofernes' designs on Judith (see also Prov 7:15-19). The reclining at table has its desired effect, as the author exploits the general's sensuality. In v.16 his heart is ravished and he seeks to possess her. As in the Amnon story, it is a question of deception. However, deception has also been Judith's strategy since her first encounter with Holofernes.

The element of irony is present here too. In v.14 Judith accepts the invitation to dine with Holofernes, adding that until her dying day this will be a constant joy. As the story unfolds, her happiest day will be Holofernes' dying day. Such joy is linked with v.18. Judith admits quite candidly that she will drink with the general because her life has taken on a meaning which it never possessed before. Life for Judith means death for Holofernes.

The day is fast approaching. The fourth day signals not only the day of the banquet but the great day in the lives of both Judith and Holofernes. The author uses the day motif to advantage. In v.18 Judith flatters Holofernes with the words: "'. . . my life means more to me *today* than in *all the days* since I was born.' " In v.20 the author remarks that Judith's ravishing beauty made Holofernes consume a huge quantity of wine, indeed "much more than he had ever drunk in any *one day* since he was born." The meaning of life and the imbibing of wine (death) come together on this one eventful day.

DEATH AND LIFE
13:1-20.

The author now has Judith carry out her strategy. Such strategy means death for Holofernes but life for Israel. The material may be divided as follows: (1) the death of Holofernes (13:1-10a); (2) departure and celebration (13:10b-20).

THE DEATH OF HOLOFERNES
13:1-10a.

13 When evening came, his slaves quickly withdrew, and Bagoas closed the tent from outside and shut out the attendants from his master's presence; and they went to bed, for they all were weary because the banquet had lasted long. ²So Judith was left alone in the tent, with Holofernes stretched out on his bed, for he was overcome with wine.

³Now Judith had told her maid to stand outside the bedchamber and to wait for her to come out, as she did every day; for she said she would be going out for her prayers. And she had said the same thing to Bagoas. ⁴So every one went out, and no one, either small or great, was left in the bedchamber. Then Judith, standing beside his bed, said in her heart, "O Lord God of all might, look in this hour upon the work of my hands for the exaltation of Jerusalem. ⁵For now is the time to help thy inheritance,

and to carry out my undertaking for the destruction of the enemies who have risen up against us."

⁶She went up to the post at the end of the bed, above Holofernes' head, and took down his sword that hung there. ⁷She came close to his bed and took hold of the hair of his head, and said, "Give me strength this day, O Lord God of Israel!" ⁸And she struck his neck twice with all her might, and severed his head from his body. ⁹Then she tumbled his body off the bed and pulled down the canopy from the posts; after a moment she went out, and gave Holofernes' head to her maid, ¹⁰who placed it in her food bag.

In a few short verses the author arranges the characters and props for the death scene. It is only fitting that all the guests — with one exception — should leave the tent. The slaves, therefore, tactfully withdraw because of the lateness of the hour (rather than "when evening came"). Next, Bagoas (historically a Persian who took part in Artaxerxes III's campaign in Egypt in 341 B.C. together with a Cappadocian prince named Holofernes) prudently closes the tent from the outside. He thereby excludes all the attendants who may have had a reason to linger in the king's presence. In turn, Judith instructs her maid to wait outside the bedroom, ostensibly in view of the usual nocturnal prayers / bath. (She is also carrying the food bag!) Most importantly, Judith communicates the same message to Bagoas in order to avoid arousing suspicion. The author notes succinctly in v.3 that Judith was alone with Holofernes in the tent (see also v.4).

Now is the hour! Given the previous descriptions of her piety, the reader is not surprised that Judith chooses to pray before striking the fatal blow. In keeping with her character, she identifies in terms of the community and thus considers her action a blow for Israel's freedom. Her work looks to the exaltation of Jerusalem. *Her* action will bring relief to *God's people*. The concluding words of the prayer underline Israel's communal concern, not Judith's personal vested interests: " '. . . carry out *my* undertaking for the destruction of the *enemies* who have risen up against *us*.' "

The Old Testament is not wanting in classical models for such death scenes. Ehud's dispatching of Eglon, the obese king of Moab (Judg 3:15-27), and David's victory over Goliath (1 Sam 17:48-54) come immediately to mind. However, Sisera's death at the hands of Jael (Judg 4:17-22; 5:24-27) offers perhaps a closer parallel. Besides the use of deceit (Jael promises to shelter Sisera), in both the Jael and Judith accounts there is a heroine who kills the national enemy singlehandedly and does so by going for the victim's head. In keeping with the David story irony demands that the culprit die by his own sword. To make the punishment fit the crime, the sword of Holofernes which was used against so many others is now the instrument of his own demise.

Judith's action is the reversal of the weak woman/strong man roles. In v.7 Judith again prays, this time for strength. To execute Holofernes, she must take hold of the hair of his head with the one hand and wield the sword with the other. Indeed, she must strike twice — hardly what one would expect of a weak woman! The reference to the bed and the canopy in v.9 reinforces the role reversal. When Judith and Holofernes first met, the general "was resting on his bed, under a canopy . . ." (10:21). Judith now tumbles his body off the bed and pulls down the canopy. The role reversal is complete with Judith's oath of innocence in v.17 which is nothing short of a victory cry. The scheming Holofernes had sought to defile and shame Judith, yet the equally scheming Judith prevented the defilement and shame by tricking him to his destruction.

DEPARTURE AND CELEBRATION
13:10b-20.

> 10b Then the two of them went out together, as they were accustomed to go for prayer; and they passed through the camp and circled around the valley and went up the

mountain to Bethulia and came to its gates. [11]Judith called out from afar to the watchmen at the gates, "Open, open the gate! God, our God, is still with us, to show his power in Israel, and his strength against our enemies, even as he has done this day!"

[12]When the men of her city heard her voice, they hurried down to the city gate and called together the elders of the city. [13]They all ran together, both small and great, for it was unbelievable that she had returned; they opened the gate and admitted them, and they kindled a fire for light, and gathered around them. [14]Then she said to them with a loud voice, "Praise God, O praise him! Praise God, who has not withdrawn his mercy from the house of Israel, but has destroyed our enemies by my hand this very night!"

[15]Then she took the head out of the bag and showed it to them, and said, "See, here is the head of Holofernes, the commander of the Assyrian army, and here is the canopy beneath which he lay in his drunken stupor. The Lord has struck him down by the hand of a woman. [16]As the Lord lives, who has protected me in the way I went, it was my face that tricked him to his destruction, and yet he committed no act of sin with me, to defile and shame me."

[17]All the people were greatly astonished, and bowed down and worshiped God, and said with one accord, "Blessed art thou, our God, who hast brought into contempt this day the enemies of thy people."

[18]And Uzziah said to her, "O daughter, you are blessed by the Most High God above all women on earth; and blessed by the Lord God, who created the heavens and the earth, who has guided you to strike the head of the leader of our enemies. [19]Your hope will never depart from the hearts of men, as they remember the power of God. [20]May God grant this to be a perpetual honor to you, and may he visit you with blessings, because you did not spare your own life when our nation was brought low, but have avenged our ruin, walking in the straight path before our God." And all the people said, "So be it, so be it!"

Lamentation now yields to exultation, narrative cedes to liturgy. Judith's appeal to the guards to open the gate of

Bethulia is like the cry in the entrance procession of Ps 24 (23):7: "Lift up, O gates, your lintels; reach up, you ancient portals! that the king of glory may come in." (See also Ps 118[117]:19; Isa 26:2.) One gets the impression that the Lord is actually accompanying Judith in her victorious return to the city.

Once all the people have gathered around Judith in the glow of the bonfire, she breaks out into a hymn of praise: "'Praise God, O praise him!'" Upon learning the story of Judith's valor and seeing the head of Holofernes, the people respond liturgicaly in v.17: "'Blessed are thou, our God,...'" Uzziah then pronounces a twofold blessing: the first is directed to Judith (vv.18a, 19-20), the second to Deborah's praise of Jael in Judg 5:24: "'Most blessed of women be Jael...'" Finally the people voice their acceptance in the conclusion: "'So be it, so be it!'"
sion: "'So be it, so be it!'"

Judith's display of Holofernes' head smacks of David's action and the Maccabean soldiers' gesture. 1 Sam 17:54 mentions that David took Goliath's head and brought it to Jerusalem. In 1 Macc 7:47 Judas Maccabeus' soldiers cut off the head and right hand of Nicanor and displayed them just outside Jerusalem. Against the background of the mid-second century B.C. *Judith's* exploit would remind readers of *Judas* Maccabeus' soldiers and their fight against Hellenism. After the manner of Holofernes' execution the author of 1 Macc 7:47 wrily notes: "and they cut off ... the right hand which he (Nicanor) had so arrogantly stretched out ..." The punishment fits the crime.

The Exodus coloring of Judith's act of bravery also appears in this chapter. Verse 15 concludes with Judith's statement that the Lord has struck down Holofernes by the hand of a woman. The end of v.14, moreover, uses the same Greek verb as Exod 15:6. Judith's motive for praise (" 'has destroyed our enemies by my hand' ") reflects the Song of the Sea (Exod 15:6): " 'thy right hand, O Lord, shatters the enemy.' " Hence Judith's hand is the Lord's instrument in crushing the neo-Egyptians, i.e., the Assyrians. The phrase

" 'this very night' " recalls the Lord's slaughter of the Egyptian first-born in Exod 12:12: " 'For I will pass through the land of Egypt that night. . .' " (See also " 'this day' " in v. 11.)

JUDITH AND HER TROOPS 14:1-19.

The author first shows Judith issuing her orders. He then moves on to consider the impact of Judith's deed on Achior. The final scene is a description of the consternation in the Assyrian camp. The material may be divided as follows: (1) Judith and her troops (14:1-4); (2) Judith and Achior (14:5-10); (3) discovery and panic (14:11-19).

JUDITH AND HER TROOPS
14:1-4.

14 Then Judith said to them, "Listen to me, my brethren, and take this head and hang it upon the parapet of your wall. ²And as soon as morning comes and the sun rises, let every valiant man take his weapons and go out of the city, and set a captain over them, as if you were going down to the plain against the Assyrian outpost; only do not go down. ³Then they will seize their arms and go into the camp and rouse the officers of the Assyrian army; and they will rush into the tent of Holofernes, and will not find him. Then fear will come over them, and they will flee before you, ⁴and you and all who live within the borders of Israel shall pursue them and cut them down as they flee.

Judith now assumes command of the army and begins to deploy her troops. These verses show Judith's tactics for the showdown against the Assyrian troops. She first arranges for displaying Holofernes' head on the parapet of the wall. The decapitation was the assurance of victory, the rest is now a question of mopping up. Then she plans the attack at daybreak in which the troops are to rush out of the city and pretend descending to the plain. At the sight of the Jewish forces the Assyrians will arouse their commander-in-chief. His headless corpse will strike fear in the Assyrians and the fear will eventually become panic. At this point it is but a question of pursuit and slaughter.

Judith does not participate in the battle itself, although she has clearly struck the decisive blow. She is like her prototype Deborah who summons Barak, accompanies him, encourages him, but assures him that the glory will belong to a woman, viz., Jael (see Judg 4:4-16). In chap. 8 Judith emerged as the seemingly frail woman who would dare to oppose Holofernes and his army. Now that army has no general whereas Israel has Judith.

JUDITH AND ACHIOR
14:5-10.

⁵But before you do all this, bring Achior the Ammonite to me, and let him see and recognize the man who despised the house of Israel and sent him to us as if to his death."

⁶So they summoned Achior from the house of Uzziah. And when he came and saw the head of Holofernes in the hand of one of the men at the gathering of the people, he fell down on his face and his spirit failed him. ⁷And when they raised him up he fell at Judith's feet, and knelt before her, and said, "Blessed are you in every tent of Judah! In every nation those who hear your name will be alarmed. ⁸Now tell me what you have done during these days."

Then Judith described to him in the presence of the people all that she had done, from the day she left until the moment of her speaking to them. [9]And when she had finished, the people raised a great shout and made a joyful noise in their city. [10]And when Achior saw all that the God of Israel had done, he believed firmly in God, and was circumcised, and joined the house of Israel, remaining so to this day.

These verses seem to be out of place. As soon as Judith finishes issuing her orders, one expects to read of their immediate executive, viz., vv.11-19. Moreover, Achior's praise of Judith and the people's response (vv.7, 9) would appear to belong to the liturgy of chap. 13. Why does the author delay the attack and have Judith summon Achior before the showdown?

Although some commentators prefer to place 14:5-10 between 13:16 and 13:17, the Achior scene seems to fit its present place. Though the sage par excellence, Achior, i.e., Ahiqar, did not succeed in convincing Holofernes in chap. 6. With the emergence of Judith there developed the wise man/foolish woman tension. At this particular point in the account, Judith has demonstrated courage and wisdom, not only in decapitating Holofernes, but also in deploying her troops to attain the maximum victory. The reader knows that the foolish woman has triumphed and can now look forward to Achior's stamp of approval.

Achior recognizes both the superior wisdom of Judith and the presence of the God of Israel in her. He now becomes a convert to Judaism by accepting circumcision. However, since Achior is an Ammonite (see 5:5), he cannot join the ranks of Israel according to Deut 23:3-4. However, while his conversion clearly violates the Torah, it does serve the purpose of encouraging proselytes. In 6:10-16 Holofernes ordered Achior to be seized, bound, and deposited at the foot of Bethulia to share the fate of the besieged Jews. The author may be contrasting the Hellenistic disdain for Judaism with the experience of salvation which Judaism brings in the person of Judith. Thus, Achior represents not an isolated pagan but the invitation to sincere pagans to come over to the God of Israel. Judith has just made the leader of the Ammonites a convert to Judaism.

The liturgy resumes. Achior pronounces Judith blessed in every tent of Judah (see Judg 5:24), adding that among the pagans merely to hear her name will occasion fear. Although the people of Bethulia knew of Judith's feat in chap. 13, they only learn the details when the heroine recites the event blow by blow to Achior. At the conclusion of the account the only adequate response is a great shout and a joyful noise.

DISCOVERY AND PANIC
14:11-19.

11As soon as it was dawn they hung the head of Holofernes on the wall, and every man took his weapons and they went out in companies to the passes in the mountains. 12And when the Assyrians saw them they sent word to their commanders, and they went to the generals and the captains and to all their officers. 13So they came to Holofernes' tent and said to the steward in charge of all his personal affairs, "Wake up our lord, for the slaves have been so bold as to come down against us to give battle, in order to be destroyed completely."

14So Bagoas went in and knocked at the door of the tent, for he supposed that he was sleeping with Judith. 15But when no one answered, he opened it and went into the bedchamber and found him thrown down on the platform dead, with his head cut off and missing. 16And he cried out with a loud voice and wept and groaned and shouted, and rent his garments. 17Then he went to the tent where Judith had stayed, and when he did not find her he rushed out to the people and shouted, 18"The slaves have tricked us! One Hebrew woman has brought disgrace upon the house of King Nebuchadnezzar! For look, here is Holofernes lying on the ground, and his head is not on him!"

19When the leaders of the Assyrian army heard this, they rent their tunics and were greatly dismayed, and their loud cries and shouts arose in the midst of the camp.

The discovery of the cadaver produces the desired effect. Bagoas' reaction, viz., that his master is sleeping with Judith, is somewhat similar to that of Eglon's servants in Judg 3:24-25, i.e., that he is relieving himself. But this initial reaction to delay soon leads to consternation and confusion. At this moment the reader recalls the irony expressed in the first meeting between Judith and Holofernes. In 11:19 Judith promised the general a throne in Jerusalem but now there is no head on which to place the crown. Judith also promised at the same time that Holofernes would lead the Jews like sheep without a shepherd. Now, of course, the Assyrians are the ones who are leaderless. The headless corpse is hardly a flattering expression of Assyrian military might.

Bagoas' lament (" 'One Hebrew woman has brought disgrace upon the house of King Nebuchadnezzar!' ") illustrates the Israelite belief that God uses the weak to confound the strong. One frail woman has wreaked greater havoc on Nebuchadnezzar than the combined military strength of the vassal nations. In vv. 13, 18 the author describes the Jews as slaves. Although the Exodus allusions should not be pressed, the author may be suggesting that Nebuchadnezzar's disgrace is the Exodus revisited. The new Pharaoh has learned what weak slaves armed only by the strength of their God can achieve. The Reed Sea has returned in the springs of Bethulia. The Lord's hand has struck once again. The weak hand of a Jewish widow has severed the greatest military leader and his army.

The liturgy in Bethulia is in contrast to the liturgy in the camp below. There are cries and shouts in the camp but they are the liturgy of lamentation. The rending of garments expresses the frustration of the Assyrians and the reversal of roles. Israel had previously directed its frustration to the Lord in the form of lamentation — hence in a form of prayer. Outside Israel, however, lamentation is an exercise in frustration. The Book of Judith dramatically illustrates the difference between Israelite prayer and pagan resignation.

THE SWEET TASTE OF VICTORY
15:1-13.

The author describes Israel's rout of the Assyrian forces. But the sweet taste of victory reminds the people of their debt of gratitude to Judith. The material may be divided as follows: (1) the military victory (15:1-7); (2) the exaltation of Judith (15:8-13).

THE MILITARY VICTORY
15:1-7.

15 When the men in the tents heard it, they were amazed at what had happened. ²Fear and trembling came over them, so that they did not wait for one another, but with one impulse all rushed out and fled by every path across the plain and through the hill country. ³Those who had camped in the hills around Bethulia also took to flight. Then the men of Israel, every one that was a soldier, rushed out upon them. ⁴And Uzziah sent men to Betomasthaim and Bebai and Choba and Kola, and to all the frontiers of Israel, to tell what had taken place and to urge all to rush out upon their enemies to destroy them. ⁵And when the Israelites heard it, with one accord they fell upon the enemy, and cut them down as far as Choba. Those in Jerusalem and all the hill country also came, for they were told what had happened in the camp of the enemy; and those in Gilead and in Galilee outflanked them with great slaughter, even beyond Damascus and its borders. ⁶The rest of the people of Bethulia fell upon the Assyrian camp and plundered it, and were greatly enriched. ⁷ And the Israelites, when they returned from the slaughter, took possession of what remained, and the villages and towns in the hill country and in the plain got a great amount of booty, for there was a vast quantity of it.

The Jewish attack is an overwhelming success. Verse 2 describes the panic and the disruption of military order. The enemy breaks ranks and scatters in all directions. Yet the reader is prepared for this breakdown in military discipline. When Judith first appeared in the Assyrian camp, "there was great excitement" (10:19). It was the heroine's great beauty which next inflamed the general and led to his demise. The present panic is the logical result of the initial breakdown. However, the Jewish success is a national effort. The distances noted in v.5 support this. Assuming that Bethulia is in the plain of Dothan opposite Esdraelon (4:6), then Jerusalem lies about forty miles to the south, Gilead about 20 miles east across the Jordan, and Damascus about 100 miles to the north. Bethulia has not won a great victory, all Israel has.

The section is also a study in reversals. According to 7:18 the Edomites and Ammonites were encamped in the hill country opposite Dothan. In v.3 these ancient enemies of Israel also flee along with the Assyrians. Ironically, only one Ammonite enjoys the security of Bethulia, viz., Achior, the Jewish convert. In 4:4 Choba fortified itself in preparation for the war against Holofernes and in 4:6 Betomesthaim seized the passes in the hills to prevent the invasion of Judea. In v.4 these two cities abandon their defensive strategy to take part in the offensive of the fleeing enemy.

The plundering is an especially ironic reversal of fortune. In 2:23, 26 Holofernes carries out Nebuchadnezzar's orders to plunder the whole region (2:11). In 4:1-2, 12 the Jews are alarmed over the possible plundering of Jerusalem and the temple. However, in 7:26 the inhabitants of Bethulia are willing to let their city be plundered. Yet Judith counters by observing that the plundering of Bethulia will lead to the plundering of the sanctuary (8:21). Ironically, the Assyrian booty is now the possession of the only people that dared to oppose King Nebuchadnezzar and his mighty general. To the victor belong the spoils.

THE EXALTATION OF JUDITH
15:8-13.

[8]Then Joakim the high priest, and the senate of the people of Israel who lived at Jerusalem, came to witness the good things which the Lord had done for Israel, and to see Judith and to greet her. [9]And when they met her they all blessed her with one accord and said to her, "You are the exaltation of Jerusalem, you are the great glory of Israel, you are the great pride of our nation! [10]You have done all this singlehanded; you have done great good to Israel, and God is well pleased with it. May the Almighty Lord bless you for ever!" And all the people said, "So be it!"

[11]So all the people plundered the camp for thirty days. They gave Judith the tent of Holofernes and all his silver dishes and his beds and his bowls and all his furniture; and she took them and loaded her mule and hitched up her carts and piled the things on them.

[12]Then all the women of Israel gathered to see her, and blessed her, and some of them performed a dance for her; and she took branches in her hands and gave them to the women who were with her; [13]and they crowned themselves with olive wreaths, she and those who were with her; and she went before all the people in the dance, leading all the women, while all the men of Israel followed, bearing their arms and wearing garlands and with songs on their lips.

Judith once more commands attention. In v.8 Joakim the high priest and the Jewish senate arrive to inspect the situation. They come to witness what the Lord has accomplished and to see Judith. Actually to see Judith is to witness what the Lord has accomplished since Judith is the Lord's instrument, strategist, and accomplice. The praise bestowed upon her in v.9 is merely recognition of what the author has stressed all along, viz., Judith's identity in terms of God's people. She is honored, not as the leading widow of Bethulia, but as Jerusalem's exaltation, Israel's glory, and the nation's pride.

Judith's hand is again emphasized. Instead of the RSV's "'singlehandedness'" in v.10 one should translate literally: "'You have done all this by your hand.'" Judith's hand has undone what Nebuchadnezzar's hand threatened to do against the vassal nations in 2:12. It is a fitting tribute to the seemingly weak hand of a seemingly weak woman.

Reversal also appears here. In 3:7 the people from Sidon, Tyre, Sur, Ocina, Jamnia, Azotus, and Ascalon (2:28) sued for peace with Holofernes and "welcomed him with garlands and dances and tambourines"(3:7). Now Israel, which alone had the courage to withstand Holofernes, dances, sings and wears garlands (vv.12-13). Holofernes' bed was to be the scene of Judith's violation. But it now becomes a war trophy for the heroine who carts it away (v.11). According to 7:20 the Assyrian army besieged Bethulia for thirty-four days. After Judith has spent four days in the Assyrian camp (12:10), the people of Israel proceed to despoil the Assyrian camp for the next thirty days (v.11).

Judith's reception in vv.15-16 smacks of David's triumphal parade following his victory over Goliath. 1 Sam 18:6-7 is a precedent: ". . . , the women came out of all the cities of Israel, singing and dancing, to meet King Saul, with timbrels, with songs of joy, and with instruments of music . . ." The only way to celebrate "Victory in Bethulia Day" is to sing, to dance, and to wear garlands. At the same time this celebration is the natural point of departure for Judith's song in chap. 16.

The Jewish victory over the Assyrians reflects the Jewish victory over the Hellenists in the second century B.C. The use of the garlands (v.13) fits the Hellenistic period since this was a Hellenistic, not a Jewish custom (see 3:7; also Wis 2:8). The Assyrian panic in vv.1-2 and the Jewish destroy mission in vv.5, 7 bear more than a passing resemblance to the Maccabean rout of General Nicanor and his Hellenistic forces in 1 Macc 7:44-50. In this connection it is interesting to note that the verb "to outflank" in v.5 appears only one more time in the Greek Bible, viz., in 1 Macc 7:46. Likewise the Greek word for "branch" (v.12) is found only once more in the Greek Bible, viz., in 2 Macc 10:7. This is connected with the Maccabean celebration of the purification of the temple in 164 B.C. This feast of Hanukkah has other links with the Book of Judith.

A FINAL TRIBUTE
16:1-25.

This chapter is a combination of prose and poetry. It begins with a prose introduction (v.1) in which Judith imitates Miriam, Moses' sister, by leading the people in song. It is possible that Judith and the people alternated in singing the song of praise. Verses 2-12 are Judith's canticle. Verses 13-17 are a collection of praise from the Psalms, the Book of Judges, and the Book of Isaiah. Finally vv.18-25 are the prose conclusion of the story. The material may be divided as follows: (1) Judith's canticle (16:1-12); (2) a collection of praise (16:13-17); (3) prose conclusion (16:18-25).

JUDITH'S CANTICLE
16:1-12.

16 Then Judith began this thanksgiving before all Israel, and all the people loudly sang this song of praise. ²And Judith said,
   Begin a song to my God with tambourines,
      sing to my Lord with cymbals.
   Raise to him a new psalm;
      exalt him, and call upon his name.
   ³For God is the Lord who crushes wars;
      for he has delivered me out of the hands
         of my pursuers,

and brought me into his camp, in the midst
of the people.

4The Assyrian came down from the mountains
of the north;
he came with myriads of his warriors;
their multitude blocked up the valleys,
their cavalry covered the hills.
5He boasted that he would burn up my territory,
and kill my young men with the sword,
and dash my infants to the ground
and seize my children as prey,
and take my virgins as booty.

6But the Lord Almighty has foiled them
by the hand of a woman.
7For their mighty one did not fall by the
hands of the young men,
nor did the sons of the Titans smite him,
nor did tall giants set upon him;
but Judith the daughter of Merari undid him
with the beauty of her countenance.

8For she took off her widow's mourning
to exalt the oppressed in Israel.
She anointed her face with ointment
and fastened her hair with a tiara
and put on a linen gown to deceive him.
9Her sandal ravished his eyes,
her beauty captivated his mind,
and the sword severed his neck.
10The Persians trembled at her boldness,
the Medes were daunted at her daring.

11Then my oppressed people shouted for joy;
my weak people shouted and the enemy trembled;
they lifted up their voices, and the enemy were
turned back.
12The sons of maidservants have pierced them through;
they were wounded like the children of fugitives,
they perished before the army of my Lord.

Since the battle against the Assyrians is the Exodus revisited, it is only fitting that the book should conclude with the hymn sung by Moses and the Israelites after Pharaoh's defeat at the Reed Sea (Exod 15:1-19). Although Judith's canticle resembles the Song of Deborah (Judg 5), in which the heroine speaks in the first person and is spoken of in the third person, the basic inspiration is Exod 15:1-19. Indeed the canticle is a summary of chaps. 8-15, hence a pulling together of all the material from the vantage point of God's / Israel's action in Egypt. When Judith sings of "me" and "my," she sings of Israel. Both the people of Bethulia and the heroine herself, i.e., all Israel, coalesce to form a corporate personality. The canticle, therefore, sings of an Israel pursued and delivered in the new Exodus in Bethulia. The canticle is a classic example of how Israel could draw from the past to interpret the needs of the present.

Judith's canticle imitates the Song of the Sea by first expressing the need to praise and then by suggesting the motives for praise. As seen in 9:7, v.3 is really Exod 15:3. The rest of the verse should read: " '. . . and set his camp among his people; he snatched me from the hands of my persecutors.' " (Actually no one pursued Judith on her return to Bethulia.) Verse 4 mentions the Assyrian war machine which reflects the Egyptian war machine in Exod 15:4 (chariots, host, picked officers). Verse 5 described Assyria's war boast which in turn interprets Exod 15:9 (the intention to pursue, despoil, and annihilate). Judith's hand (v.6) corresponds to Yahweh's right hand mentioned in Exod 15:6.

On the other hand, there are differences between the two songs. Exod 15:17 introduces a geographical shift, viz., the Lord's own sanctuary, whereas v.5 remains confined to Bethulia. Verse 4 identifies the enemy as the Assyrians whereas v.10 adds the Persians and the Medes. (In 1:7 Nebuchadnezzar invited the Persians to join in the war against Arphaxad.) In Exod 15:14-15 fear strikes the Philistines, Edomites, Moabites, and Canaanites. The reference, therefore, to the Persians and Medes reflects the reference to the Song of the Sea. The Persians and Medes, however, are not distinct from the Assyrians since their fate is the same as that of the Assyrians. Although the author has employed Exod 15 to advantage, he has not copied it slavishly.

The canticle restates in poetic form several of the key points of the prose story. For example, v.5 repeats Judith's identification with Israel's suffering. As a widow, she can express Israel's vicissitudes. Verse 6 hammers home once again the theology of weakness/strength, woman's hand/ Lord Almighty. Verse 9 captures in poetry the prose description of Judith's astonishing beauty. The verbs "to ravish" and "to captivate" sum up her overall effect. The reference to her sandal is reminiscent of Cant 7:1: "How graceful are your feet in sandals, O queenly maiden!" Since the sandals left the top part of the foot bare, the effect on Holofernes' eyes is understandable.

A COLLECTION OF PRAISE
16:13-17.

13I will sing to my God a new song:
    O Lord, thou art great and glorious,
        wonderful in strength, invincible.
14Let all thy creatures serve thee,
        for thou didst speak, and they were made.
    Thou didst send forth thy Spirit, and it formed them;
there is none that can resist thy voice.
15For the mountains shall be shaken to their
        foundations with the waters;
        at thy presence the rocks shall melt like wax,
    but to those who fear thee
        thou wilt continue to show mercy.
16For every sacrifice as a fragrant offering
        is a small thing,
        and all fat for burnt offerings to thee is a
        very little thing,
    but he who fears the Lord shall be great for ever.
17Woe to the nations that rise up against my people!
    The Lord Almighty will take vengeance on

them in the day of judgment;
fire and worms he will give to their flesh;
they shall weep in pain for ever.

These verses are a collection of praise and lack the overall impact of vv. 2-12. Yet they do interpret the story. Verse 14 offers a theology of God's creative word as found, e.g., in Ps 33 [32]:6. God's "spirit" is God's breath functioning as speech or voice. Once God decided to act against the Assyrians, his creative breath was as effective as against the chaos of Gen 1:1. The disruption of nature in v.15 and the woe addressed to the pagans in v.17 suggest the Song of Deborah (Judg 5:4-5, 31) and thus cast Judith as the new female warrior. Verse 16 borrows from Ps 51 [50]:16 and the wisdom literature in general. Verse 17 is from the conclusion of the Book of Isaiah (Isa 66:24). They convey the sense of allegiance to Yahweh and Yahweh's acceptance of that allegiance by action against the enemy.

PROSE CONCLUSION
16:18-25.

[18]When they arrived at Jerusalem they worshiped God. As soon as the people were purified, they offered their burnt offerings, their freewill offerings, and their gifts. [19]Judith also dedicated to God all the vessels of Holofernes, which the people had given her; and the canopy which she took for herself from his bedchamber she gave as a votive offering to the Lord. [20]So the people continued feasting in Jerusalem before the sanctuary for three months, and Judith remained with them.

[21]After this every one returned home to his own inheritance, and Judith went to Bethulia, and remained on her estate, and was honored in her time throughout the whole country. [22]Many desired to marry her, but she remained a widow all the days of her life after Manasseh her husband died and was gathered to his people. [23]She became more and more famous, and grew old in her husband's house,

until she was one hundred and five years old. She set her maid free. She died in Bethulia, and they buried her in the cave of her husband Manasseh, [24]and the house of Israel mourned for her seven days. Before she died she distributed her property to all those who were next of kin to her husband Manasseh, and to her own nearest kindred. [25]And no one ever again spread terror among the people of Israel in the days of Judith, or for a long time after her death.

Verses 18-20 recount the liturgical celebration in Jerusalem. Verse 18 is reminiscent of the celebration in Jerusalem following the siege of that city in 701 B.C.: "And many brought gifts to the Lord to Jerusalem and precious things to Hezekiah king of Judah . . ." (2 Chr 32:23; see Jdt 15:11). The plundering of chap. 15 takes on a further dimension of irony in v. 19. Judith dedicates not only the vessels of Holofernes which the people had given her in 15:11 but also the trophy she had taken for herself — the bed canopy. This symbol of the bedroom and hence the would-be place of violation has now come full circle: from Holofernes to Judith and from Judith to the Lord.

The three-month feasting in Jerusalem may be another link with the feast of Hanukkah. According to the chronology of the book (see 2:27; 3:10; 7:20; 12:10; 15:11) it is possible that the pilgrims arrived in Jerusalem around the end of September or the beginning of October for the feast of Tabernacles and stayed until Hanukkah. According to 2 Macc 10:6 the Jews celebrated the first Hanukkah as joyfully as Tabernacles. According to the festal letter in 2 Macc 1:9 the Jews in Egypt are to celebrate Tabernacles in the month of Chislev, i.e., the month in which Hanukkah falls.

Verses 21-25 are what one would expect from a heroine of Judith's stature. She continues to remain faithful to the memory of Manasseh, although desirable suitors are obvious plentiful. Like Job and the patriarchs, she dies at a ripe old age — a clear blessing from the Lord for her heroism on behalf of Israel. The seven-day funeral celebration (see Sir 22:12) evokes the memory of Judith's daring exploit for Israel.

Before dying, however, Judith continues to be both pious and dutiful. In v.23 she releases the maid who shared in her dangerous move to the Assyrian camp. In accordance with Num 27:5-11 she disperses her property to the next of kin of her husband Manasseh. The final verse is a fitting tribute to the tenor of the whole book, viz., Judith's identification in terms of Israel, not herself. The peace which Judith won for her people continued even after her death. Yet Judith continued to live because Israel continued to live.

The Book of Tobit

CONTENTS

INTRODUCTION TO
THE BOOK OF TOBIT

The Appeal of the Book

The Book of Tobit is a study in Jewish family life. It relates the fortunes of two such families in exile. Tobit, although originally successful, loses his position, is reduced to poverty, and despite his obvious piety is afflicted with blindness. In another area of the Diaspora Sarah too has to cope with tragedy. She has lost seven husbands in a row —all killed on the occasion of their wedding night. The book weaves the piety of such families into a story which becomes a model for Jewish existence and faith in the midst of adversity.

The book stands in stark contrast to Judith. Tobit reflects the vicissitudes of two families while Judith looks to the fate of the Jewish nation. In Tobit the two families join together in a brave effort to ward off further tragedy while in Judith the reaction to tragedy is the call, not less brave but surely more vindictive, to arms. Tobit reflects the courageous acceptance of pain while Judith provides the heroic expression of direct conflict. In Tobit the story revolves around the journey of the son, Tobias, while in Judith it focuses on the military expertise of the female warrior.

The Book of Tobit unfolds the drama of two little people, Tobit and Sarah, pitted against a system of apparent fate and a seemingly disinterested God. Both protagonists are concerned with the meaning of life in the demanding world of the Diaspora. They are wondering about the maze of their own existence, attempting to work out a rationale in God's erratic behavior. At the same time these little people are giants because they communicate a sense of humor in the most painful situations. For example, in 5:13 Tobit must examine the family tree of Raphael alias Azarias, although the reader knows that Raphael is really an angel.

Yet Tobit and Sarah are more than God's afflicted in Assyria and Media. They are Israel. They represent the desired response to God's word. They are models for Jewish behavior, compelling the Jewish audience to adopt their courageous example and so transform their lives. Tobit is not another harmless Jewish story. It is an object lesson in the manner of persevering Israelite faith.

The Setting of the Book

Tobit is an exile from the northern kingdom who is forced to settle in Nineveh, the Assyrian capital. Although his brethren give themselves up to pagan practices, Tobit clings tenaciously to his Israelite faith. Because of that faith the Assyrian king, Shalmaneser V (726-722 B.C.), makes him a prosperous purchasing agent who often travels to Media where he leaves a considerable deposit with his kinsman, Gabael. Later a citizen of Nineveh reports him to another Assyrian king, Sennacherib (704-681 B.C.), for burying the bodies of those Israelites whom the same king has slain. As a result, Tobit is forced to go into hiding and is left with nothing except his wife Anna and his son Tobias. However, owing to his nephew's (Ahiqar) intercession with the next Assyrian king, Esarhaddon (680-669 B.C.), Tobit is able to return to Nineveh.

Once again tragedy strikes. He persists in burying the bodies of slain kinsmen. After one such episode he sleeps outside in his courtyard because of the heat. Unfortunately bird droppings land on his uncovered face, resulting in blindness, a condition which lasts a number of years. Because of his financial plight his wife Anna has to work for hire at weaving cloth. On one occasion she returns home with a bonus from her employers only to hear that her husband suspects her of stealing. This remark so infuriates her that she begins to question the reasonableness of his good deeds. Chap. 3 opens with a very depressed Tobit.

The rest of the story is the quest for the fortune deposited with Gabael and its effect on the two families. It describes the journey of the son Tobias in the company of Raphael, an angel in disguise. There is a stop in Ecbatana in Media where Tobias meets unfortunate Sarah. Owing to Raphael's medical expertise Sarah is able to survive the wedding night. Raphael then proceeds to recover the deposit from Gabael in Rages, picks up Tobias and Sarah, and returns to Nineveh. Raphael's medical skill now results in the restoration of Tobit's sight. Finally Raphael must depart but reveals his identity before returning to heaven. Tobit then lives happily ever after. Sarah, moreover, becomes the mother of seven sons. In the final scene Tobias leaves Nineveh at his father's advice and settles in Media at Ecbatana. Virtue triumphs once again.

Because of space limitations this commentary will examine only chaps. 3, 6, 8, 11, and 14. However, the thrust of the story will be briefly indicated at each point.

Origins and Literary Form

Folklore has had its impact on Tobit. An obvious folk tale is the story of the bewitched bride. Sarah's string of seven unfortunate husbands is calculated to introduce God's intervention through Raphael and so unite the two plagued families.

Another contribution from folklore is the colorful Ahiqar who enjoyed a reputation for wisdom in the ancient Near East. His popularity is evident from the many different forms of his story, including a fifth century B.C. Aramaic text from the Jewish colony in Elephantine (near modern Aswan) in Egypt. Since Ahiqar was the trusted counsellor of both King Sennacherib and King Esarhaddon, it seemed only fitting for the author of Tobit to introduce him as a nephew of Tobit, thereby enhancing the latter's status. Although Ahiqar is mentioned only four times in the book, his presence lends an atmosphere of ancient wisdom to the story. When Tobit offers sound advice on coping and serving God (see chaps. 4, 14), the reader must conclude that such wisdom is part of the family tradition (see also Raphael in chap. 12) The Ahiqar tradition also provides the background of the successful courtier in which the fortunes and reverses of Tobit and his nephew Ahiqar become the vehicle for articulating a theology of history.

The most obvious influence on the book is the Old Testament itself. The author clearly dialogues with his scriptural heritage and adapts it to the needs of his audience. For example, the wedding night in chap. 8 is a blend of Gen 2 and Israel's prayer style. The quest for a bride for Tobias in chaps. 6, 7 is modelled on the quest for a bride for Isaac in Gen 24. Prophetic texts, such as Isa 60, exert a considerable influence on the description of the new Jerusalem (see chap. 13).

By far the greatest single influence on Tobit is the Book of Deuteronomy. For example, exile and destruction of "the Good Land" are due to infidelity and apostasy (see Deut 28:15-68; Tob 14:4). However, even after judgment there is the possibility of mercy (see Deut 30:1-4; Tob 14:5-6). The only legitimate place for the Lord's worship is the Jerusalem Temple (see Deut 12:1-14; Tob 14:5, 7). Tobit may be called "Deuteronomy Revisited" since the story reflects the living out of the covenant implications of that book.

Angels and demons add to the color and theological message of the story. Gen 18-19 is an example of angels in disguise who demonstrate God's ongoing concern with his created world. In Tobit, however, the angel has a proper name — Raphael. The author develops angelic intervention against demons by having Raphael interact against the wicked Asmodeus. Angelology/demonology is a significant departure from Judith where only humans occupy center stage and thus control the destiny of others.

As in Esther and especially Judith, there are certain incongruities which rule out sober history as the literary genre. According to 1:2 Tobit was taken captive by Shalmaneser V (726-722 B.C.), whereas the deportation of the region was the work of Tiglath-pileser (744-727 B.C.) in 733 B.C. (see 2 Kgs 15:29). In 1:15 Sennacherib is represented as the son of Shalmaneser V, whereas the latter's real son was Sargon II (722-705 B.C.). The two-day journey from Rages to Ecbatana (5:6) is actually a trek of some 185 miles. Despite 1:4 the division of the Davidic-Solomonic kingdom occurred in 931 B.C. This hardly harmonizes with the notice of 14:5 according to which Tobias dies after the fall of Nineveh (612 B.C.). Tobit is not scientific history.

Some see Tobit as the union of wisdom and an edifying or didactic story. Other suggest popular romance. Unlike Esther and especially Judith, it does not have something of an historical nucleus to qualify it as an historical novel. Perhaps it is best to label it a religious novel whose aim is to teach and edify. This would account for the emphasis on wisdom and traditional practices such as prayer and almsgiving.

The Author's Purpose

The Book of Tobit, precisely as a religious novel, is intended to reinforce fidelity to the Lord. It speaks to a Jewish community in need of hope and consolation. The focus on Nineveh and Media suggests a Diaspora audience, although it also applies to the Palestinian community. Both groups suffered from pagan influence. For the author, Israel's past offers lessons for coping in the present. Deuteronomy's doctrine of fidelity/prosperity and infidelity/disaster is judged to be a viable theology of history for the ongoing covenant community. At a time when Jews wondered about the meaning of their faith and its application to the present crisis, the author's message is clear: dare to be different. He urges them not to conform to pagan practices but to translate the heritage of Israel into day by day covenant living. To be a covenant people means to be different.

At the same time the author seeks to inculcate that sense of joy which comes from covenant faith. Where there is responsibility, there is the presence of a concerned Lord. The author, therefore, seeks to embody the history of Israel in the lives of the two principal characters, Tobit and Sarah. He retraces salvation history in the ups and downs of these committed people. When despair and discouragement seem the order of the day, the Lord of the covenant is not aloof. He is especially present through the concern of fellow Jews — hence the emphasis on such practices as almsgiving. Jewish commitment to Yahweh is measured by Jewish commitment to the community of Yahweh.

Time of Composition

The existence of the Second Temple (515 B.C.) appears to be presupposed in 14:5. In the other direction there are no allusions to the Maccabean wars which were so much in evidence in the Book of Judith. A majority of authors suggest the period between 200 and 170 B.C. as the time of composition and see the threat to Jewish faith as coming from the allurements of Hellenism. However, the finding of almost half the text of Tobit at Qumran may point to an earlier date. In view of this a date in the third century B.C. should not be ruled out. The place of composition is unknown.

Like the Book of Judith, the Book of Tobit is a deuterocanonical work whose canonical language is Greek. However, the Greek goes back to a Semitic original. Because of the Aramaic fragments from Qumran there is now greater support for regarding that language as the original one.

The Greek text exists in three different forms. The form

used by the RSV (Vaticanus and Alexandrinus — the "shorter" text) does not represent the best reading of the Semitic original. Thus the JB, NEB, and NAB have chosen another form (Sinaiticus — the "longer" text) as their basic text. Whenever the RSV has to be corrected, this is indicated by placing "NAB" in parentheses.

Jerome's Vulgate is a somewhat unique witness to the original Aramaic. Its uniqueness may be due to the oral transmission of that original. On occasion an addition from the Vulgate will be cited. Because of differences between the Latin and Greek texts the verse numbering is often different and will be noted.

LAMENTATION AND RESPONSE 3:1-17.

After describing Tobit's plight in chaps. 1-2, the author narrates his lament, culminating in a request for death. He now presents Sarah's humiliation and subsequent lament. However, God hears the prayers of both and responds by sending Raphael. The material may be divided as follows: (1) the lamentation of Tobit and Sarah (3:1-15); (2) God's response (3:16-17).

THE LAMENTATION OF TOBIT AND SARAH 3:1-15.

3 Then in my grief I wept, and I prayed in anguish, saying, [2]"Righteous art thou, O Lord; all thy deeds and all thy ways are mercy and truth, and thou dost render true and righteous judgment for ever. [3]Remember me and look favorably upon me; do not punish me for my sins and for my unwitting offenses and those which my fathers committed before thee. [4]For they disobeyed thy commandments, and thou gavest us over to plunder, captivity, and death; thou madest us a byword of reproach in all the nations among which we have been dispersed. [5]And now thy many judgments are true in exacting penalty from me for my sins and those of my fathers, because we did not keep thy commandments. For we did not walk in truth before thee. 6And now deal with me according to thy pleasure; command my spirit to be taken up, that I may depart and become dust. For it is better for me to die than to live, because I have heard false reproaches, and great is the sorrow within me. Command that I now be released from my distress to go to the eternal abode; do not turn thy face away from me."

7On the same day, at Ecbatana in Media, it also happened that Sarah, the daughter of Raguel, was reproached by her father's maids, 8because she had been given to seven husbands, and the evil demon Asmodeus had slain each of them before he had been with her as his wife. So the maids said to her, "Do you not know that you strangle your husbands? You already have had seven and have had no benefit from any of them. 9Why do you beat us? If they are dead, go with them! May we never see a son or daughter of yours!"

10When she heard these things she was deeply grieved, even to the thought of hanging herself. But she said, "I am the only child of my father; if I do this, it will be a disgrace to him, and I shall bring his old age down in sorrow to the grave." 11So she prayed by her window and said, "Blessed art thou, O Lord my God, and blessed is thy holy and honored name for ever. May all thy works praise thee for ever. 12And now, O Lord, I have turned my eyes and my face toward thee. 13Command that I be released from the earth and that I hear reproach no more. 14Thou knowest, O Lord, that I am innocent of any sin with man, 15and that I did not stain my name or the name of my father in the land of my captivity. I am my father's only child, and he has no child to be his heir, no near kinsman or kinsman's son for whom I should keep myself as wife. Already seven husbands of mine are dead. Why should I live? But if it be not pleasing to thee to take my life, command that respect be shown to me and pity be taken upon me, and that I hear reproach no more."

What's in a name? Everything! "Tobit" is a shortened form of "Tobiah." Both names mean: "Yahweh is good." ("Tobias" is the Greek form of "Tobiah.") In view of the family's misfortunes, one can legitimately raise the question: is Yahweh really good? The conclusion of the story, however, vindicates the use of such names. (See 1:1 for Tobit's grandfather [Ananiel —"God is merciful"] and his father [Tobiel — "God is good"].)

Although Tobias and Anna (Tobias' mother) are important in the story, the real protagonists are Tobit and Sarah ("princess"). Chap. 3 calls attention to their problems by highlighting the language of lamentation. As in the Exodus account (see Exod 2:23-24; 3:6; 6:5), lamentation directs God's attention to the implications of covenant. Since God has promised to look after the needs of his people, he is necessarily involved in the plight of Tobit and Sarah. The implication of lamentation is that it should be a growth experience. Coping with frustration and despair should lead one to a new awareness of the God of the covenant and, in turn, his claim on their lives. It is only fitting that the reaction to the resolution of pain should be praise (see 13:2-18). By chap. 14 Tobit and Sarah are different people — they will have grown in the process of lament and praise.

Tobit and Sarah have similar problems which demand God's immediate attention. For both of them the number seven is significant. This is obvious in Sarah's loss of seven husbands. But Tobit also has seven calamities: (1) deportation (1:2, 10); (2) confiscation of property in exile (1:19-20); (3) blindness (2:10); (4) Anna's wrath (2:14 — not unlike Job's wife in Job 2:9-10); (5) depression (3:1-6); (6) concern for Tobias during his absence (10:1-3); (7) Anna's cutting remark about Tobias' absence (10:7).

Both Tobit (v.6) and Sarah (v.13) long for death, in fact Sarah has even contemplated the possibility of suicide (v.10). Both desire the listless existence of Sheol, the underworld, for their present life is really death. To be "in extremis" is to court death. The ridicule experienced by both Tobit and Sarah confirms this deathlike existence. In 2:8 Tobit's neighbors mock him for burying the dead; in 2:14 Anna belittles him for the lack of return from his good deeds. In vv.8-9 one of Sarah's maids (different in RSV) scorns her for her marriage record, adding the wish for the continuation of zero child production. (It is the exact opposite of the wish expressed by Edna, Sarah's mother, later in the story: " '. . . , and grant me to see your children by my daughter Sarah . . .' " [10:12].)

Despite such reverses both Tobit and Sarah continue to demonstrate faith and hope. As seen in chaps. 4 and 14, Tobit will be the new Moses who will twice address the audience in farewell speeches. His sound advice smacks of similar speeches by Moses in Deuteronomy. Sarah will be the new Sarah, the latter-day counterpart of Abraham's wife. She will become a mother after all and thus manifest God's power to intervene and save. The God who delivered Sarah from the harems of Pharaoh (Gen 12:10-20) and Abimelech (Gen 20:1-17) will save this Sarah from the grip of the demon.

The influence of Deuteronomy is evident. The covenantal language finds expression in God's attributes in v.2: righteous, merciful, truthful. In this context God reveals his righteousness by showing mercy. "Truthful" (see also v.5) implies authenticity, reliability, genuineness. Verses 2-5 reflect Deuteronomy's theology of retribution: virtue brings material prosperity but wickedness brings material disaster (see Deut 7:12-16; 28:1 ff.). Tobit believes that his virtue will ultimately triumph, even though he suffers at the present. (Such a theology spawned its own critics, e.g., Job and Qoheleth.)

"Remembering" (v.3) is also very much at home in Deuteronomy (see Deut 7:18; 8:2, 18). It connotes making the record of past relationships with God have an impact on the present in view of the future. "To remember" is to have the radical capacity to believe that help will be forthcoming.

The expression "byword" (v.4), especially in connection with exile, is another link with Deuteronomy. Covenantal infidelity makes Israel a parade example of Yahweh's justice in the setting of captivity (see Deut 28:37). In a few verses the author prepares for Tobit as a latter-day Moses.

The author of Tobit cannot accept a theology of fate. He endeavors to point out that happenings, even bizarre ones, are somehow part of God's intricate plan. In such a theology only providence, not chance, is acceptable.

In 2:9 the author binds together the elements of heat, lack of protection, and affliction. Because of the heat in Nineveh Tobit did not cover his face and was thereby afflicted with blindness as a result of the bird droppings. In turn, blindness will relate to the journey of Tobias and Raphael and the subsequent recovery of sight.

In v.7 the author notes that "on the same day" as Tobit experienced depression in Nineveh, Sarah was victim of despair in Ecbatana. In v.10 "that day" (NAB) when Tobit was overcome with grief, Sarah was similarly affected. In v.11 the author continues that "at that time" (NAB) Sarah prayed and in v.16 "at that very time" (NAB) God heard the prayers of both Tobit and Sarah. Finally in 3:17 "at the very moment" Tobit reentered his house, Sarah descended from her room. The overlapping of events in Nineveh and Ecbatana demonstrates the author's concern to establish Yahweh's covenantal involvement and to make both Tobit and Sarah models of faith for the Jewish audience (see also 4:1).

GOD'S RESPONSE
3:16-17.

> [16]The prayer of both was heard in the presence of the glory of the great God. [17]And Raphael was sent to heal the two of them: to scale away the white films from Tobit's eyes; to give Sarah the daughter of Raguel in marriage to Tobias the son of Tobit, and to bind Asmodeus the evil demon, because Tobias was entitled to possess her. At that very moment Tobit returned and entered his house and Sarah the daughter of Raguel came down from her upper room.

The author now introduces Raphael. Once again names articulate theology. Raphael means: "God heals." According to 5:12-13 Raphael's supposed lineage is impressive:

Azarias ("Yahweh helps"), Ananias ("Yahweh is merciful"), Jathan ("Yahweh gives"), and Shemaiah ("Yahweh hears"). In terms of God's providing for Tobit and Sarah the list is in reverse order. Yahweh first hears the prayer and is then disposed to give. God is first moved to mercy and only then offers concrete help in the mission of Raphael. The last intervention is the healing of both Tobit and Sarah.

In 12:15 the author identifies Raphael as one of the seven angels who communicate the prayers of the faithful to God. In 12:19 he states that Raphael only appeared to eat and drink. For the author, therefore, angelology plays a significant role in God's providence. The angel makes God present and thus reveals a wholly interested God. This is like Gen 16:9-13 and Num 22:22-35 where the messenger and God are ultimately identified as one and the same person.

In v.17 the author announces the healings and then goes on to mention the Asmodeus/Raphael bout. "Asmodeus" is a Persian term meaning "demon of wrath" (in Aramaic it is known as "the Destroyer"). The author is now preparing his audience for a final contest: will "the Destroyer" be able to match and overcome "God heals"?

According to the RSV Raphael's task is to bind the evil demon Asmodeus. According to the better reading of 3:17, however, Raphael's mission is to set Sarah free (NEB; "drive" in NAB) from the evil demon Asmodeus. The expression "to set free" is used in Aramaic divorce texts which in turn depend on older ancient Near Eastern materials. Against this setting Raphael functions as an exorcist. He is called upon to pronounce the divorce between the evil demon Asmodeus and Sarah. In these texts, before proceeding to the actual rites, the exorcist must acknowledge that a given deity has confided this mission to him, otherwise the demon(s) may turn against the exorcist. Raphael's declaration in 12:14, 20 is somewhat in keeping with this ancient exorcist tradition: " 'So now God sent me to heal you and your daughter-in-law Sarah, . . . , I am ascending to him who sent me.' " The angel-exorcist of Tobit is similar to the angel-scribe and the angel-architect in Ezek 9:2; 40:3.

Since the overcoming of blindness is one of the central features of the book, it is not surprising that the author employs the motif of light. In 3:17 and 5:10 (NAB) Tobit is described as being unable to see God's sunlight. In 7:7 Raguel, Tobit's kinsman, is distressed when he learns of his blindness. In 3:6 (NAB) Tobit observes that it is better to die than to see so much misery in life. It is hardly by chance that both Tobit and Sarah use the language of sight in their prayers: " 'look favorably upon me' " (v.3) and " 'command that respect be shown,' " i.e., " 'look kindly upon me' " (v.15). Tobit's new sight will actually mean insight into the operations of God's providence. To see again is to acknowledge that Yahweh is indeed good and to attest that the name Tobit/Tobias is meaningful.

RAPHAEL: PHYSICIAN AND MATCHMAKER
6:1-17.

In chap. 4 Tobit addresses a farewell speech to his son which is replete with maxims about charity, almsgiving, temperance, etc. He then instructs Tobias to reclaim the money deposited with his kinsman Gabael at Rages in Media. In need of a knowledgeable traveling companion Tobias "happens" to come upon Raphael who, using the alias of Azarias, offers his services to Tobias. The success of the venture is assured when Tobit consoles his distraught wife with the words: " 'For a good angel will go with him; his journey will be successful, and he will come back safe and sound' " (5:21).

The traveling team consists of three: Raphael, Tobias, and the dog. Although the dog is wanting in the RSV text (but see NAB 6:2), it will appear later in 11:4. The presence of the dog is at odds with Old Testament usage since such animals figured mainly as scavengers and occasionally as watchdogs (see Isa 56:10). The warm relationship between Tobias and the dog is more at home in Greco-Roman literature where the dog was regularly a household animal. In Tobit the dog shares the experience of his master, including the return home.

In this chapter Raphael lives up to his name by functioning as a physician. However, his expertise also extends to matchmaking.

6 Now as they proceeded on their way they came at evening to the Tigris river and camped there. ²Then the young man went down to wash himself. A fish leaped up from the river and would have swallowed the young man; ³and the angel said to him, "Catch the fish." So the young man seized the fish and threw it up on the land. ⁴Then the angel said to him, "Cut open the fish and take the heart and liver and gall and put them away safely." ⁵So the young man did as the angel told him; and they roasted and ate the fish.

And they both continued on their way until they came near to Ecbatana. ⁶Then the young man said to the angel, "Brother Azarias, of what use is the liver and heart and gall of the fish?" ⁷He replied, "As for the heart and the liver, if a demon or evil spirit gives trouble to any one, you make a smoke from these before the man or woman, and that person will never be troubled again. ⁸And as for the gall, anoint with it a man who has white films in his eyes, and he will be cured."

⁹When they approached Ecbatana, ¹⁰the angel said to the young man, "Brother, today we shall stay with Raguel. He is your relative, and he has an only daughter named Sarah. I will suggest that she be given to you in marriage, ¹¹because you are entitled to her and to her inheritance, for you are her only eligible kinsman. ¹²The girl is also beautiful and sensible. Now listen to my plan. I will speak to her father, and as soon as we return from Rages we will celebrate the marriage. For I know that Raguel, according to the law of Moses, cannot give her to another man without incurring the penalty of death, because you rather than any other man are entitled to the inheritance."

¹³Then the young man said to the angel, "Brother Azarias, I have heard that the girl has been given to seven husbands and that each died in the bridal chamber. ¹⁴Now I am the only son my father has, and I am afraid that if I go in I will die as those before me did, for a demon is in love with her, and he harms no one except those who approach her. So now I fear that I may die and bring the lives of my father and mother to the grave in sorrow on my account. And they have no other son to bury them."

¹⁵But the angel said to him, "Do you remember the words with which your father commanded you to take a wife from among your own people? Now listen to me, brother, for she will become your wife; and do not worry about the demon, for this very night she will be given to you in marriage. ¹⁶When you enter the bridal chamber, you shall take live ashes of incense and lay upon them some of the heart and liver of the fish so as to make a smoke. ¹⁷Then the demon will smell it and flee away, and will never again return. And when you approach her, rise up, both of you, and cry out to the merciful God, and he will save you and have mercy on you. Do not be afraid, for she was destined for you from eternity. You will save her, and she will go with you, and I suppose that you will have children by her." When Tobias heard these things, he fell in love with her and yearned deeply for her.

The chapter provides interesting details from folklore which serve to articulate the theological message. While bathing in the Tigris, Tobias is attacked by a fish. However, the possible danger is changed into a pharmaceutical miracle. The gall, heart, and liver were reputed to have healing power even among the medical authorities of antiquity. Fumigation was also regarded as a practical means of driving away demons. According to vv.16-17 the fumigation takes effect even prior to the prayer of the young couple. The combined use of magic and medicine comes under the aegis of God's providence in the story. The fish was no accident, just as Raphael, the medical expert, was no accident. The journey has indeed had a very auspicious beginning.

Besides serving as a medical authority, Raphael is also the matchmaker. The purpose of the journey is not merely to fetch some money but also to win a wife, specifically Raguel's daughter (v.12). When Tobias objects that the demon's exclusive love for Sarah is lethal for all would-be husbands (v.14), Raphael reveals his expertise in the fine art of love and magic.

In the spirit of Deuteronomy (see Deut 7:18; 8:2; 9:7) Raphael asks Tobias whether he remembers (v.15) his father's previous instructions about marrying one of his own kind (4:12). Raphael then elaborates the order of events on the wedding night: (1) expulsion of the demon; (2) communal prayer; (3) intercourse. (In the Vulgate [6:16-22] St. Jerome's text reads more like a commentary, calling for three nights of prayer and chastity, since those who forget God and give themselves up to physical desire are in the demon's power.) Raphael adds persuasiveness to his arsenal of talents. In the end Tobias is not only willing to follow his advice but he proceeds to fall in love with Sarah even before seeing her.

The biblical model for seeking a bride is Gen 24 where Eliezer (Gen 15:2) at the request of Abraham sets out for Nahor in Aram Naharaim. The trusted employees in this marital enterprise bear similar names: Eliezer ("My God is help") and Azarias ("Yahweh helps"). As if by accident, but actually by God's design, Eliezer is led to the house of his master's kinsmen (Gen 24:27), although Raphael knows his destination in advance (v.10). In both instances the prospective bride is a beautiful virgin (Gen 24:16; Tob 3:8, 14; 6:12). Last, but certainly not least, the marriage is one made in heaven: " '. . . , for she was destined for you from eternity' " (v.17; see Gen 24:14). (For further use of this model compare Tob 7:8-10, 11, 12-14, 15 with Gen 24:31-32, 33, 51, 54.)

While Tobias already loves Sarah, the chapter subordinates such love to a higher system of values, viz., the obligations of family and kinship. Tobias' objection to the proposed marriage (v.14) is grounded in his concern for his parents. He is afraid that the almost certain death awaiting him will merely cause undue pain and sorrow to his parents. Earlier in 3:10 Sarah had contemplated suicide by hanging but relented because of the disgrace this would cause her father. Her chastity (3:15) is a tribute to her father's name. Now Tobit must marry Sarah since he is the only eligible kinsman and family obligation is a higher law (v.11). Similarly Sarah is obliged to marry Tobias (see 7:12) and keep

Raguel's property in the family since he has no other heir (3:15; 6:11; Num 36:8-9). Although v.12 calls for the death penalty for disobedience, the Old Testament itself does not stipulate such.

The happiness of the family will be the happiness of the couple. By thinking within the framework of the family's needs, both Tobias and Sarah appear as models of family loyalty. Their personal needs are subordinated to the needs of others. Self-fulfillment thereby implies self-emptying. As the story turns out, their self-empyting will enrich both households.

EXORCISM, PRAYER, AND CELEBRATION
8:1-21.

In chap. 7 Raphael and Tobias arrive at Raguel's house in Ecbatana. Raguel receives them warmly and is enthusiastic upon learning that Tobias is Tobit's son. When Raphael explains the purpose of their visit, viz., to have Sarah marry Tobias, Raguel insists that they join him for a meal. Tobias, however, presses the issue until Raguel consents, even writing out a proper legal document. The chapter closes with Edna leading her daughter Sarah into the oft ill-fated bedroom.

In chap. 8 the author first narrates the effective exorcism. This then leads to Tobias' prayer. Fearing the worst, Raguel prepares to dig the grave. However, he is informed of the successful exorcism and begins a prayer of praise and thanksgiving. The conclusion is the wedding celebration. The material may be divided as follows: (1) the successful exorcism (8:1-3); (2) Tobias' prayer (8:4-9a); (3) Raguel's reaction (8:9b-18) the wedding celebration (8:19-21).

THE SUCCESSFUL EXORCISM
8:1-3.

8 When they had finished eating, they escorted Tobias in to her. ²As he went he remembered the words of

Raphael, and he took the live ashes of incense and put the heart and liver of the fish upon them and made a smoke. ³And when the demon smelled the odor he fled to the remotest parts of Egypt, and the angel bound him.

"God heals" triumphs over "the Destroyer." The greek historian Herodotus mentions that after intercourse with his wife, a Babylonian husband sits down before a censer of burning incense with his wife opposite him. In the Tobit story the fumigating powers of the fish's heart and liver produce the desired effect — the Destroyer's flight. However, flight is not enough. To ensure containing the demon's influence, Raphael embarks on a journey of some 2000 miles to Upper Egypt. The area suggests the desert which in the biblical record is a traditional haunt of demons (see Isa 13:21; 34:14). There Raphael binds Asmodeus — the Destroyer is thereby destroyed. The notion of binding a demon is a traditional one. Aramaic texts speak about demons who are chained with their hands and feet tied. In Mk 5:5 the local community attempted to control the Gerasene demoniac with fetters and chains.

TOBIAS' PRAYER
8:4-9a.

⁴When the door was shut and the two were alone, Tobias got up from the bed and said, "Sister, get up, and let us pray that the Lord may have mercy upon us." ⁵And Tobias began to pray,
"Blessed art thou, O God of our fathers,
and blessed be thy holy and glorious name for ever.
Let the heavens and all of thy creatures bless thee.
⁶Thou madest Adam and gavest him Eve his wife
as a helper and support.
From them the race of mankind has sprung.
Thou didst say, 'It is not good that the man
should be alone;
let us make a helper for him like himself.'
⁷And now, O Lord, I am not taking this sister of mine

because of lust, but with sincerity. Grant that I may find
mercy and may grow old together with her." [8]And she
said with him, "Amen." [9]Then they both went to sleep for
the night.

Tobias' prayer reflects the author's attitude toward marriage. He quotes the creation account in Gen 2:18-25. However, he makes an addition to the text. The wife is not only a
help but also a support. The language of the Genesis
account is clearly covenantal, i.e., it is a question of communal dedication, not the individual advantage of the husband.
(" 'Bone of my bones and flesh of my flesh' " means abiding
loyalty through thick and thin.) Here Tobias states that he
takes his sister, viz., his beloved — his wife, not because of
lust but " 'with sincerity.' " "Sincerity" translates the Greek
word "truth," a covenantal term which connotes authenticity, reliability, genuineness (see 3:2, 5). Tobias exhibits such
"truth" by carrying out the obligation to marry within the
tribe, etc. Hence covenantal authenticity prompts him to
marry Sarah, not sexual gratification.

The anxiety has given way to praise and supplication.
Tobias suggests that God should be consistent with his plan.
Since Sarah and he are part of that plan, they have a claim
on God's mercy. Furthermore, their married love should
also continue until their old age. God should see through
whatever he begins.

The presumption is that Tobias and Sarah consummated
their marriage after the prayer. The note in v.9 (that they
went to sleep after the prayer) and v.13 (that the maid found
them both asleep) should be linked with the subsequent
wedding celebration. The celebration presumes the consum-
mation of the marriage, although Jerome recommends
three days of abstinence.

RAGUEL'S REACTION
8:9b-18.

[9b]But Raguel arose and went and dug a grave, [10]with the
thought, "Perhaps he too will die." [11]Then Raguel went

into his house [12]and said to his wife Edna, "Send one of the maids to see whether he is alive; and if he is not, let us bury him without any one knowing about it." [13]So the maid opened the door and went in, and found them both asleep. [14]And she came out and told them that he was alive. [15]Then Raguel blessed God and said,

"Blessed art thou, O God, with every pure
   and holy blessing.
Let thy saints and all thy creatures bless thee;
let all thy angels and thy chosen people
   bless thee for ever.
[16]Blessed art thou, because thou hast made me glad.
   It has not happened to me as I expected;
   but thou hast treated us according to
   thy great mercy.
[17]Blessed art thou, because thou hast had compassion
   on two only children.
Show them mercy, O Lord;
   and bring their lives to fulfilment in health
   and happiness and mercy."
[18]Then he ordered his servants to fill in the grave.

Raguel also breaks out into prayer. He employs the same type of logic as Tobias. This demonstration of concern towards Tobias and Sarah should merely anticipate greater blessings to come: " 'and bring their lives to fulfilment in health and happiness . . .' " (v.17).

God's name matches the reality. In v.7 Tobias asks God's mercy on his married life. In v.16 Raguel ("God is a friend") acknowledges that he has received God's great mercy and thus the proof of divine friendship. For the author the Lord has simply vindicated the divine claims in the names of the people in the story. For example, Tobit's grandfather's name, Ananiel (1:1), means "God is merciful." Raphael's father's name, Ananias (5:12), means "Yahweh is merciful." In the theology of Tobit, for God to bear a name is to be that name.

Deuteronomic elements also appear. In v.2 Tobias remembers Raphael's words — Tobias thus has the capacity to believe that help will somehow be forthcoming in an otherwise desperate situation. Joy is another Deuteronomic feature. Moses instructs the people to rejoice in the good things God has provided for them (see Deut 12:7, 18, 14:26; 20:6). Covenantal fidelity must reveal itself in joy. Thus Raguel proclaims that God has made him glad (v.16). In v.20 (NAB) Raguel instructs Tobias to bring joy to Sarah's downcast spirit.

Raguel's abortive burial plans reflect a motif in the book. Tobit's practice of burying the dead results in confiscation of property (1:16-20) and blindness (2:1-10). Tobit instructs his son to bury him (4:3) — a charge which Tobias executes in **14:11. In turn, both Tobias (6:14) and Sarah (3:10) mani**fest concern over causing pain to parents and thus not providing a proper burial. Significantly the filling in of Tobias' would-be grave (v.18) demonstrates God's intent to provide for the faithful. The man who dug graves for others does not merit to have a premature grave dug for his son (see 12:13). The disempowering of Asmodeus by means of the wonder drugs also suggests the disempowering of Tobit's blindness by means of the remaining medicine. Paradoxically, graves are linked, not only with death, but also with life.

THE WEDDING CELEBRATION
8:19-21.

> [19]After this he gave a wedding feast for them which lasted fourteen days. [20]And before the days of the feast were over, Raguel declared by oath to Tobias that he should not leave until the fourteen days of the wedding feast were ended, [21]that then he should take half of Raguel's property and return in safety to his father, and that the rest would be his "when my wife and I die."

The fourteen-day wedding feast (v.21) expresses different features of the author's theology. In keeping with the injunction of Deuteronomy (see Deut 12:12; 14:26; 16:11) it manifests covenantal joy, but an unprecedented one (a wedding feast usually lasted seven days —see Gen 29:27). It also corroborates the name theology of Tobit's great-grandfather, Aduel (1:1), which means "God is joy." It also suggests the empowering/disempowering motif of banquets in Esther. The celebration connotes the disempowering of the demon Asmodeus and the empowering of Tobias and Sarah to take their rightful place in Israel as parents.

A number theology also appears. Tobit's seven calamities and Sarah's seven calamities have given way to a fourteen-day celebration. Sarah's seven calamities are reversed by her bearing seven sons to Tobias (14:3 — NAB, a reading supported by the Old Latin Version [14:5] and one of the Qumran manuscripts).

TOBIAS' RETURN
AND TOBIT'S SIGHT
11:1-19.

Chap. 10 narrates, first of all, the anxiety of Tobias' parents. The delay causes hardship for both Tobit and Anna, but especially for Anna. She gets no sleep at all, crying throughout the night. She would wait by the road each day, hoping to catch a glimpse of her son. The chapter then switches to the departure from Ecbatana. At the end of the fourteen-day celebration Raphael, Tobias, and Sarah must leave for Nineveh. This departure scene contains admonitions relating to family life.

Chap. 11 focuses on two returns: (1) the return of Tobias from Ecbatana; (2) the return of sight to Tobit. The expected response is one of praise.

11 After this Tobias went on his way, praising God because he had made his journey a success. And he blessed Raguel and his wife Edna.

So he continued on his way until they came near to Nineveh. [2]Then Raphael said to Tobias, "Are you not aware, brother, of how you left your father? [3]Let us run ahead of your wife and prepare the house. [4]And take the gall of the fish with you." So they went their way, and the dog went along behind them.

[5]Now Anna sat looking intently down the road for her son. [6]And she caught sight of him coming, and said to his

father, "Behold, your son is coming, and so is the man who went with him!"

⁷Raphael said, "I know, Tobias, that your father will open his eyes. ⁸You therefore must anoint his eyes with the gall; and when they smart he will rub them, and will cause the white films to fall away, and he will see you."

⁹Then Anna ran to meet them, and embraced her son, and said to him, "I have seen you, my child; now I am ready to die." And they both wept. ¹⁰Tobit started toward the door, and stumbled. But his son ran to him ¹¹and took hold of his father, and he sprinkled the gall upon his father's eyes, saying, "Be of good cheer, father." ¹²And when his eyes began to smart he rubbed them, ¹³and the white films scaled off from the corners of his eyes. ¹⁴Then he saw his son and embraced him, and he wept and said, "Blessed art thou, O God, and blessed is thy name for ever, and blessed are all thy holy angels. ¹⁵For thou hast afflicted me, but thou hast had mercy upon me; here I see my son Tobias!" And his son went in rejoicing, and he reported to his father the great things that had happened to him in Media.

¹⁶Then Tobit went out to meet his daughter-in-law at the gate of Nineveh, rejoicing and praising God. Those who saw him as he went were amazed because he could see. ¹⁷And Tobit gave thanks before them that God had been merciful to him. When Tobit came near to Sarah his daughter-in-law, he blessed her, saying, "Welcome, daughter! Blessed is God who has brought you to us, and blessed are your father and your mother." So there was rejoicing among all his brethren in Nineveh. ¹⁸Ahikar and his nephew Nadab came, ¹⁹and Tobias' marriage was celebrated for seven days with great festivity.

Verse 15 expresses the Deuteronomic doctrine of retribution: God has scourged (afflicted) but now he shows mercy. Fidelity necessitates the restoration of sight. The view of Deuteronomy is that Yahweh not only inflicts wounds but also heals (see Deut 32:39). If Israel will cry out to Yahweh, as Tobit did, then Yahweh will hear and change Israel's lot (see Deut 30:1-4; Tob 13:6).

Tob 13:2-6 also spells out this doctrine of retribution but implies (see 13:9) that, while God afflicts Jerusalem for the wickedness of her sons, he will again take pity on the sons of the righteous. In 12:14 Raphael announces that God sent him to test (NAB) Tobit. Moreover, since Tobit has walked in the path of righteousness all the days of his life (see 1:3), his suffering must be probationary, not the result of any sinfulness.

The author of Tobit lacks the perception of the author of Job. While Job's friends try to console him with the theory of probationary suffering (see Job 5:17; Prov 3:11-12), Job rejects their advice categorically (see Job 13:1-13). Job concludes that his suffering is part of his relationship with El Shaddai and that dimension is cloaked in mystery (see Job 38:1—42:6). The author of Tobit, on the other hand, happily accepts the Deuteronomic equation of: righteousness/ material prosperity, wickedness/material disaster.

The author returns to the light/sight motif discussed in chap. 3. In 5:21 Tobit assures his wife that her eyes will one day see the return of Tobias (NAB). In 10:7 Tobias confides to Raguel that his parents do not believe that they will ever see him again. Here in v.7 Raphael states that Tobit's eyes will be opened, adding in v.8 that he will be able to see the light of day (NAB). When Anna greets her son, she exclaims in v.9 that she is ready to die because she has seen Tobias (see Gen 46:30; Lk 2:29-30). In v.14 Tobit is ecstatic that he can see Tobias, " 'the light of my eyes' " (NAB). Tobit concludes this first outburst of joy in v.15 with the exclamation: " 'I see my son Tobias!' " As Tobit makes his way to greet Sarah, the onlookers are amazed that he can see (v.16). In v.17 before such onlookers Tobit confesses that God has mercifully restored sight to his eyes (NAB).

The recovery of sight is not merely the result of proper medical procedures. It is, rather, the sacrament of God's abiding covenantal care of his people. (Not to restore Tobit's eyesight is also to disappoint the reader). Here the author has adroitly employed his name theology. When Tobit remarks in v.15 that he can see his son Tobias, the author implies that Tobit can *see that Yahweh is good.* The emphasis on the light/sight motif is intended to demonstrate to the audience that trust and fidelity will be requited. The truly blind are those who choose not to recognize Yahweh by fidelity and serve him by meeting the needs of others. In the end Tobit sees on a new level. He is not the same as the Tobit of the beginning. He has been transformed by the experience of frustration and thus has gained sight/insight on a new level of being.

The happiness of the occasion cannot contain itself. In v.15 Tobit (Tobias in RSV) goes back into the house *rejoicing.* In v.16 he then goes out of the house *rejoicing* on his way to greet his daughter-in-law. In v.17 the joy becomes contagious among the Jewish community of Nineveh. In v.18 Tobit's nephew Ahiqar (not mentioned since 2:10) and his nephew Nadab come *rejoicing* (NAB) to Tobit's house. In v.19 there is the seven-day wedding celebration. In the Vulgate Jerome enhances this dimension of joy by noting that the dog (11:4) ran before the travelers, fawning and wagging its tail. The recovery of sight, the return of a son, the acquisition of a daughter-in-law, and regaining of a deposit all demand the proper Deuteronomic expression, viz., the command to rejoice.

Another Deuteronomic element is praise. The Israelite who witnesses God's ongoing goodness must break out in songs of praise and thanksgiving (see Deut. 8:10; 32:3, 43). To praise is to enter into the rhythm of creation and acknowledge the implications of names, viz., that God is good, very good. Thus, to see God's goodness in the very act of seeing is to acknowledge: "'Blessed art thou, O God, and blessed is thy name for ever, . . .'" (v.14). Upon reentering the house (v.15), Tobit praises God with a full voice (NAB). When going out to the gate of the city, Tobit again recognizes God's abiding concern. Not to be able to break out into praise of God is to confine oneself to a hell of individualism and isolation. Covenant demands praise.

DISCOURSE AND DEPARTURE 14:1-15.

In chap. 13, after the wedding celebration Tobit instructs his son to pay Raphael his wages and even to add a bonus, i.e., half of everything Tobias brought back. When Raphael is summoned, he proceeds to lecture Tobit and Tobias on the necessity of praising God and the efficacy of good deeds, especially almsgiving. Raphael then reveals his identity. He observes that he presented the prayers of Tobit and Sarah to the Lord. Tobit's charity in burying the dead prompted God to dispatch Raphael to heal both suppliants. Chap. 13 concludes with Raphael's ascension to heaven.

Chap. 13 is Tobit's song of praise. In the first part, vv.1-8, he sings of God's goodness, endorsing the Deuteronomic doctrine of retribution and urging wayward Israelites to repent. In the second part, vv.9-18, he addresses the new and ideal Jerusalem, making use of such prophetic texts as Isa 60.

Chap. 14 deals with the remainder of Tobit's life, his farewell speech, the death of Tobit and Anna, and finally Tobias' departure from Nineveh. The material may be divided as follows: (1) Tobit's farewell discourse (14:1-11a); (2) death and departure (14:11b-15).

TOBIT'S FAREWELL DISCOURSE
14:1-11a.

14 Here Tobit ended his words of praise. ²He was fifty-eight years old when he lost his sight, and after eight years he regained it. He gave alms, and he continued to fear the Lord God and to praise him. ³When he had grown very old he called his son and grandsons, and said to him, "My son, take your sons; behold, I have grown old and am about to depart this life. ⁴Go to Media, my son, for I fully believe what Jonah the prophet said about Nineveh, that it will be overthrown. But in Media there will be peace for a time. Our brethren will be scattered over the earth from the good land, and Jerusalem will be desolate. The house of God in it will be burned down and will be in ruins for a time. ⁵But God will again have mercy on them, and bring them back into their land; and they will rebuild the house of God, though it will not be like the former one until the times of the age are completed. After this they will return from the places of their captivity, and will rebuild Jerusalem in splendor. And the house of God will be rebuilt there with a glorious building for all generations for ever, just as the prophets said of it. ⁶Then all the Gentiles will turn to fear the Lord God in truth, and will bury their idols. ⁷All the Gentiles will praise the Lord, and his people will give thanks to God, and the Lord will exalt his people. And all who love the Lord God in truth and righteousness will rejoice, showing mercy to our brethren.

⁸"So now, my son, leave Nineveh, because what the prophet Jonah said will surely happen. ⁹But keep the law and the commandments, and be merciful and just, so that it may be well with you. ¹⁰Bury me properly, and your mother with me. And do not live in Nineveh any longer. See, my son, what Nadab did to Ahikar who had reared him, how he brought him from light into darkness, and with what he repaid him. But Ahikar was saved, and the other received repayment as he himself went down into the darkness. Ahikar gave alms and escaped the death-trap which Nadab had set for him; but Nadab fell into the trap and perished. ¹¹So now, my children, consider what almsgiving accomplishes and how righteousness delivers."

Before taking up the farewell discourse, the author devotes v.2 to describe the remainder of Tobit's life. He notes that his lifestyle is remarkably consistent: almsgiving, fear of God, praise.

Farewell discourses are at home in both the Old and New Testaments (see Gen 49:1-33; Josh 23-24; Jn 13:31-16:33; Acts 20:17-38). A person about to die offers words of hope and encouragement to family and kinsmen concerning the future. The discourse is a type of last will and testament in which the dying person elaborates guidelines to provide for the success and happiness of the bereaved. Since legal observance is often central to such guidelines, it is not surprising that Tobit's farewell discourse is permeated with Deuteronomic theology.

The discourse repeats Deuteronomic notions previously mentioned. In v.7 those who love the Lord naturally express themselves in paroxysms of joy (see Deut 12:12). In v.9 (NAB) Tobit commands his family to bless God's name "with all their strength," a phrase which derives from the Great Commandment in Deut 6:5. In vv.7 and 9 (NAB) Tobit speaks of remembering God, so that the past may bear on the present in view of the future. In vv.4-6 Tobit articulates the Deuteronomic teaching regarding the possibility of mercy in the wake of sin and judgment, indeed a mercy which will touch not only Israel but also the nations.

Deuteronomy stresses long life in the good land and fidelity-related success (see Deut 4:40). Deuteronomy also promises rest and security in the Promised Land (see Deut 12:10-11). Verse 4 refers to Israel as " 'the good land' " (see Deut 1:35; 3:25; 4:21, 22). Verses 4-5 apply the Deuteronomic doctrine of retribution. The RSV text in v.4 (see also v.8) presents Jonah as the prophet who predicted the downfall of Nineveh (see Jonah 3:4) whereas the better text (NAB) uses Nahum, the prophet who gloated over Nineveh's defeat or imminent demise in 612 B.C. In v.7 (NAB) the repentant Israelites will return to Jerusalem and dwell securely in Abraham's land forever while the unrepentant disappear from the land.

One of the hallmarks of Deuteronomy is fear and love of God. Loving Yahweh means fearing him which is then expressed concretely in keeping his commandments (see Deut 6:5, 13). In v.6 Tobit "predicts" that the Gentiles will also fear God in truth. In v.7 he designates the rejoicing community as " 'all who love the Lord God in truth and righteousness.' " In v.9 the RSV text reflects the Deuteronomic thrust by speaking of the law and the commandments. The better text (NAB), however, speaks of serving the Lord in truth.

Deuteronomy also insists on the centralization of cult, i.e., that the Jerusalem temple is the only place where Israelites may lawfully worship the Lord (see Deut 12:1-14; 16:6). In v.5, therefore, Tobit "predicts" that the house of God will be rebuilt for all generations to come (see link with Tob 1:4-5). Whereas in Tobit's day his kinsmen used to worship Jeroboam's calf (see Tob 1:5), in the future even the Gentiles will offer proper worship by abandoning their idols (v.6).

Verses 9-11a are Tobit's final exhortation. They are reminiscent of the speech in Deut 30:19-20 where Moses offers his people the choice of life or death. In v.11 Tobit insists on the good effects of almsgiving and the baneful effects of wickedness (NAB). In v.9 the author is also careful to repeat the three important notions of mercy, righteousness, and truth (this last in NAB) and thus establish a link with the beginning of the book (1:3; see also 3:2). In effect, Tobit encourages his community to follow his own example. The dying Tobit is a latter-day Moses.

To illustrate the centrality of almsgiving, Tobit cites the example of his nephew Ahiqar. In the Ahiqar story the sage adopts his nephew Nadab and grooms him to take over his position at the Assyrian court. Nadab, however, attempts to kill his uncle but in the end Ahiqar is vindicated and the nephew perishes. Ahiqar's almsgiving, especially in the case of his Uncle Tobit (see 2:10), delivered him from death.

DEATH AND DEPARTURE
14:11b-15.

> As he said this he died in his bed. He was a hundred and fifty-eight years old; and Tobias gave him a magnificent funeral. [12]And when Anna died he buried her with his father.
>
> Then Tobias returned with his wife and his sons to Ecbatana, to Raguel his father-in-law. [13]He grew old with honor, and he gave his father-in-law and mother-in-law magnificent funerals. He inherited their property and that of his father Tobit. [14]He died in Ecbatana of Media at the age of a hundred and twenty-seven years. [15]But before he died he heard of the destruction of Nineveh, which Nebuchadnezzar and Ahasuerus had captured. Before his death he rejoiced over Nineveh.

Tobit dies the way a patriarch should. He is surrounded by his son and his grandsons. After the seven calamities which befell both Sarah and himself, he can now count seven (the better reading) grandsons. Like Job (see Job 42:16), he has lived to a ripe old age. In view of his respect for the dead it is only fitting that he receive a proper burial. Virtue triumphs in the end.

As the dutiful son, Tobias receives his due reward: family, inheritance, longevity. In accordance with his father's word (v.4) he leaves Nineveh and settles in Ecbatana. Although Nabopolassar and Cyaxares, not Nebuchadnezzar and Xerxes, conquered Nineveh in 612 B.C., Tobias is able to rejoice at the fall of the city. This concluding remark is somewhat illogical since according to vv.6-7 all the Gentiles will be converted and fear the Lord. However, the attitude regarding Nineveh reflects a typical biblical stance which the Book of Jonah will legitimately question.

The Book of Jonah

CONTENTS

INTRODUCTION TO THE BOOK OF JONAH

The Appeal of the Book

If the snake has all the lines in Gen 3, then the fish appears to be center stage in Jonah. Although the author mentions the fish only three times (1:17; 2:1, 10), this three-day and three-night hostel has not failed to arouse the interest of readers and pique the imagination of artists. The swallowing and regurgitating monster of the deep has added an unforgettable dimension to the book.

But much more exciting than the fish is the prophet himself. Although Jonah is found among the twelve minor prophets in the Hebrew Bible, the author never labels him a prophet as such. When compared with the other minor prophets, Jonah occupies a unique place in the prophetic literature. While these other books contain the words of woe and/or weal pronounced by God's spokespersons, the Book of Jonah consists of only five Hebrew words (see 3:4) spoken by Jonah to his audience. While the other books refer only occasionally to the personal lives of the minor prophets (see Amos 7:10-17), the Book of Jonah is fundamentally an account of this prophet's personal adventures and exploits. While these other prophetic works reflect God's word to Israel, the Book of Jonah concentrates solely on God's word to pagans. Although prophets such as Jeremiah were reluctant to accept their prophetic mission, only Jonah attempts to elude the all-present God by means of a voyage to the far west.

It is obvious that Jonah abounds in idiosyncrasies. However, it is at the same time a challenge to exercise freedom. The Book of Jonah dares the reader to be truly free. The reader must observe the lengths to which a prophet will go in refusing to exercise concern for others, here the people of Nineveh. The reader must also note the reluctance displayed by Jonah in finally carrying out his prophetic call. The reader must thereby perceive the limitations the prophet will place on God's ability to give. The reader is thus challenged to opt either for or against such a prophetic lifestyle.

In raising the question of freedom, the book provokes a further question: will the reader recognize himself/herself in the antics of Jonah? Hence the author addresses, not only his postexilic audience, but also his modern audience. Are we Jonah? Are we the heirs of the reluctant prophet in our life setting? Do we dare to talk back to the Lord and suggest further limitations on his plan for mercy? Are we the latter-day version of copping out and fleeing the real scene? Do we recognize ourselves in Jonah?

The Setting of the Book

The author borrows his principal character from a real biblical prophet. According to 2 Kgs 14:25 Jonah, the son of Amittai from Gath-hepher in Galilee, proclaimed a message of hope and prosperity for the kingdom of Israel during the reign of Jeroboam II (793-753 B.C.). His contemporary was the prophet Amos who countered Jonah's positive message with the negative proclamation of the end of the kingdom of Israel. About fifty years after the mission of these two prophets the Assyrians destroyed that kingdom (722 B.C.).

By using the name "Jonah" (meaning "dove"), the author realizes that his audience will immediately connect the Jonah of his prophetic book with the Jonah of the eighth century B.C. He, therefore, presents a prophet who ultimately sets out to preach repentance and deliverance to the hated Assyrians. Nineveh, the Assyrian capital from about the beginning of the eighth century B.C., connoted war, oppression, and brutality. Nineveh was the quintessence of insolence and unbridled inhumanity, a verdict attested by Zeph 2:13-15; Jdt 1:1; Tob 14:4, 15; and especially the Book of Nahum. To think that God would send a prophet to offer Nineveh the chance to repent seemed the greatest folly, if not the greatest contradiction. By choosing Nineveh, the author suggests the worst form of pagan life.

The story itself disproves the apparent folly and contradiction. Pagans — first the sailors and then the Ninevites —prove to be models of piety and contrition. On the other hand, Jonah's example leaves more than a little to be desired. Jonah's father's name, Amittai (1:1), means "faithfulness." It is ironic that the pagans demonstrate more faithfulness than this "son of faithfulness."

In chaps. 1-2 God threatens both the sailors and Jonah with destruction. However, God revokes his destruction when they respond to him in prayer. The sailors and Jonah conclude by offering Yahweh due worship. In chaps. 3-4 God confronts the Ninevites and Jonah with a crisis. In the crisis of destruction the Ninevites make a response of repentance, in the crisis of non-destruction (sparing the Ninevites) Jonah makes a response of anger and regret. Finally God replies to the Ninevites' repentance by calling off the destruction and to Jonah's anger and regret by seeking a change of heart and mind.

Origins and Literary Form

Jonah is a collection of strange happenings. Not only the Ninevites but also the beasts join in the lamentation and penance (3:8). After being swallowed whole by the large fish, Jonah is unaffected by its gastric juices, is moved to pray, and is deposited safe and sound seventy-two hours later on dry land. The conversion of the Ninevites is total and instantaneous, yet the Assyrian archives are silent about the success of the prophet from Israel. A plant springs up in one day large enough to provide shade and then perishes as quickly as it sprang up. Happenings such as these suggest that the author is not bent upon providing strict history.

Some believe that to opt for something else, i.e., other than strict history, is to imperil revelation. Although such a view obtained for a considerable length of time, its defenders are few today. We realize, for example, that the parables of Jesus can offer greater insight into revelation than strict history. While it is easier to say what Jonah is not, it is more difficult to say what literary form it follows.

Allegory, parable, satire, short story, short story in the form of a parable, satirical/didactic short story — these are among the common attempts to label the literary form of the Book of Jonah. Allegory is an extended metaphor where the individual elements of the account have a hidden or figurative meaning, e.g., the swallowing refers to the Babylonian exile. However, the patterns for such an interpretation are not clear. Like the parable, Jonah is didactic. But unlike the parable, Jonah begins with an historical personage and the didactic element extends to many details.

Jonah may be safely called a short story. While it is not satire, it does contain satire, e.g., it makes Jonah appear ridiculous. It is a short story which aims at teaching. The teaching or didactic thrust is especially evident in the questions (see 1:6, 8, 10, 11; 4:4, 9, 11). As will be mentioned below, it aims at teaching God's absolute right to give.

Besides the historical Jonah of 2 Kgs 14:25, the book also employs traditions about the prophet Elijah of the ninth century B.C. Like Jonah (albeit for different reasons), Elijah flees and seeks an end to his life (see 1 Kgs 19:4). Chap. 2 is probably a preexisting psalm which the author of Jonah worked into his composition. The "fish story" was not unlikely a fable which was at home in the port city of Jaffa — a fable which has many details in common with the Indian and Greek versions of the sea monster. The author of Jonah successfully combines all these elements into a theological masterpiece.

The Author's Purpose

The author is obviously critiquing his audience. In writing about Jonah, he is writing about them, pointing out the incongruities in their own conduct. Like Jonah, this audience has taken to flight and articulated its complaints against the Lord. This audience, furthermore, refuses to yield, is given over to self-pity, and indulges in anger. Finally, this audience would be happy to die. What is the author attempting to say to such a disspirited group?

A rather common view is that the author strikes a blow against the narrow nationalism of the postexilic community, especially in the wake of the reforms of Ezra and Nehemiah. The faith of Israel, therefore, welcomes all people, even the hated Ninevites. Another view is that the author proves the possibility of a change of heart for both God and humans. Like Ezek 18:21, and more so Jer 18:1-10, Jonah offers a message of repentance: God will change, if people (even the people of Ninevah) will change.

While the Book of Jonah deals with repentance, it is not simply the fact of repentance, but the recipients of repentance, viz., Nineveh, the acme of inhumanity. This suggests more than repentance. While the Book of Jonah speaks of the conversion of Nineveh, that conversion is against a wider background. The author of Jonah strives to support God's absolute right to give. God will not be coerced by people such as Jonah into limiting his compassion. God is absolutely free to be compassionate. God retains the right to be God and therefore to be free (see Eccles 1:13; 3:10; 5:17), i.e., free to give.

The Book of Jonah is a protest against a theology of rigid conformity wherein imbalance and disharmony are cured by the appropriate dosage of retribution. While allowing for the Deuteronomic theology of conversion, Jonah lobbies against the Deuteronomic doctrine of retribution since it shackles God's freedom to give. The Book of Jonah refuses to program God and thereby precludes a computerized version of Yahweh. The God of this author retains the sovereign liberty to be a God of surprises. God's immutability is not allowed to become the fetish of human manipulation. The Book of Jonah is ultimately a story which stresses the dimension of mystery and rejoices at God's absoluteness in giving, even to the hated Ninevites.

Time of Composition

Authors often place the Book of Jonah in the Persian period (539-332 B.C.). If regarded as a reaction to the nationalistic policies of Ezra and Nehemiah (cir. 450-400 B.C.), it would be a work of the late fifth or early fourth century B.C. Recently, however, there has been a swing towards the sixth century. Some would link its teaching on repentance with the preaching of Jeremiah and Ezekiel. Some would connect this same teaching with the postexilic community of the late sixth century and its need for a change of heart.

If one grants the description of the audience as given to self-pity and indulging in anger as well as the author's intent to reinstate God's freedom, a period around 475-450 B.C. is not unreasonable. Jonah would thus be a contemporary of the prophet Malachi. It is significant that the questions raised by Malachi's audience (Mal 1:2-5; 2:17; 3:14-15) reflect the malaise of Jonah's audience.

FLIGHT IN THE FACE
OF PROPHETIC MISSION
1:1-16

The author takes up Jonah's call immediately only to report an immediate rejection. He then focuses on the storm and its resolution. With regard to the call Yahweh and Jonah are the protagonists, whereas in the storm account the captain and sailors interact with Yahweh and Jonah. The material may be divided as follows: (1) call and flight (1:1-3); (2) storm and resolution (1:4-16).

CALL AND FLIGHT
1:1-3.

> **1** Now the word of the Lord came to Jonah the son of Amittai, saying, ²"Arise, go to Nineveh, that great city, and cry against it; for their wickedness has come up before me." ³But Jonah rose to flee to Tarshish from the presence of the Lord. He went down to Joppa and found a ship going to Tarshish; so he paid the fare, and went on board, to go with them to Tarshish, away from the presence of the Lord.

After the prophetic introduction of v.1 the author has Yahweh summon Jonah to arise and go to Nineveh. The expression "arise and go" (see also 3:2) is reminiscent of the prophet Elijah whom the Lord dispatched to Zarephath (1 Kgs 17:9) and Samaria (1 Kgs 21:18).

Jonah's action is a reaction. Instead of complying, he flees. The reader may wonder at this point if Jonah's flight is spontaneous. The author holds the reader in suspense, indicating only in 4:2 that this was not Jonah's first encounter with the Lord. Joppa, the modern Jaffa, was the Mediterranean port which served Jerusalem (see 2 Chr 2:16). It is from here that the prophet books passage for Tarshish. The threefold repetition of Tarshish is not without significance. Tarshish (located on the southwestern coast of Spain) was the farthest western limit; it was moreover a place of some luxury and security (see Isa 66:19; Ezek 27:12). Although instructed to go east to Nineveh, the prophet heads west to Tarshish. His flight is not simply a pleasure cruise but a flight from God's presence. Although it was impossible to escape Yahweh's omnipresence, Jonah appears to have chosen a place where he would be sheltered from God's relentless word and where he might enjoy a modicum of peace and security. Jonah has opted for himself.

STORM AND RESOLUTION
1:4-16.

> ⁴But the Lord hurled a great wind upon the sea, and there was a mighty tempest on the sea, so that the ship threatened to break up. ⁵Then the mariners were afraid, and each cried to his god; and they threw the wares that were in the ship into the sea, to lighten it for them. But Jonah had gone down into the inner part of the ship and had lain down, and was fast asleep. ⁶So the captain came and said to him, "What do you mean, you sleeper? Arise, call upon your god! Perhaps the god will give a thought to us, that we do not perish."
> ⁷And they said to one another, "Come, let us cast lots, that we may know on whose account this evil has come upon us." So they cast lots, and the lot fell upon Jonah. ⁸Then they said to him, "Tell us on whose account this evil has come upon us. What is your occupation? And

whence do you come? What is your country? And of what people are you?" ⁹And he said to them, "I am a Hebrew; and I fear the Lord, the God of heaven, who made the sea and the dry land." ¹⁰Then the men were exceedingly afraid, and said to him, "What is this that you have done!" For the men knew that he was fleeing from the presence of the Lord, because he had told them.

¹¹Then they said to him, "What shall we do to you, that the sea may quiet down for us?" For the sea grew more and more tempestuous. ¹²He said to them, "Take me up and throw me into the sea; then the sea will quiet down for you; for I know it is because of me that this great tempest has come upon you." ¹³Nevertheless the men rowed hard to bring the ship back to land, but they could not, for the sea grew more and more tempestuous against them. ¹⁴Therefore they cried to the Lord, "We beseech thee, O Lord, let us not perish for this man's life, and lay not on us innocent blood; for thou, O Lord, hast done as it pleased thee." ¹⁵So they took up Jonah and threw him into the sea; and the sea ceased from its raging. ¹⁶Then the men feared the Lord exceedingly, and they offered a sacrifice to the Lord and made vows.

In this chapter the author uses three words which will appear again and again in his narrative: *great, cry, evil.* In v.2 Nineveh is the great city. Moreover, in v.4 there is a great (in RSV "mighty") tempest (see also v.12). Similarly the sailors experience great (in RSV "exceedingly") fear (see vv.10, 16). In v.2 the Lord instructs the prophet to cry against Nineveh. In v.6 the captain orders Jonah to cry (in RSV "call") to his God while in v.14 the crew cries to the Lord. In vv.7 and 8 the storm is considered an evil. In v.2 the evil (in RSV "wickedness") of Nineveh has come to the Lord's attention. All of these terms are significant for the author's opening scenes. Moreover, evil/wickedness seems to demand Yahweh's punitive measures.

The author has carefully structured the motifs in chap. 1 to balance those in chap. 2. There is, first of all, a crisis in the form of the storm (v.4). The crisis then elicits a response from the pagan sailors, viz., prayer (v.14). Next Yahweh reacts to the prayer by deliverance, i.e., the cessation of the storm (v.15). Finally the sailors acknowledge Yahweh's reaction by offering sacrifices and vows (v.16).

The author has also employed the element of fear to great advantage. In v.5 the sailors experience fear because of the storm. After uncovering Jonah as the cause or occasion of the calamity, they badger him with questions. In v.9 he replies that he fears the Lord. The recitation is a sincere but rote confession (yet sufficient to trigger a faith response). Ironically the prophet qualifies the Lord as the maker of the sea and the dry land — in the story Jonah will know the Lord first as the maker of the sea and only later as the maker of the dry land. In v.10 the sailors manifest great fear. They link the present danger with Jonah's reluctance to comply with the Lord's word. Finally in v.16 they come full circle in their conversion by acknowledging Yahweh by sacrifice and vows. The pagan sailors have progressed to faith whereas the Israelite prophet persists in unrepentance.

Jonah's trek is always downward. In v.3 he goes down to Joppa and eventually goes onboard (literally: "he went down") the ship. In v.5 while the sailors are jettisoning wares to lighten the ship, Jonah has already gone down to its hold. Finally in 2:4 Jonah notes that he has gone down to the nether world. While the sailors pray for life in the face of death, Jonah is willing to risk his life and the lives of the sailors rather than comply with the Lord's mission. Unlike 4:3, 8 he does not yet welcome death. However, he does view this going down to the nether world as more reasonable than preaching to the Ninevites.

The author is careful to point out that Yahweh who instigated the problem at sea continues to control the outcome of the event. The verb "to throw" thus becomes a theological tool. In v.4 God throws (in RSV "hurled") a raging wind upon the sea. In v.5 the sailors throw over the cargo. In v.12 Jonah acknowledges that the storm is the result of his noncompliance and hence urges the sailors to throw him into the sea. Finally in v.15 the sailors do throw him overboard and the storm abates. When one attempts to avoid God's word for others, God intervenes. The throwing of the prophet into the raging sea is proof that the Lord still exercises his freedom for the good of others. God chooses to need Jonah for the sake of the Ninevites.

Irony is not wanting in these two scenes. First the prophet abandons his prophetic mission and then proceeds to fall asleep in the midst of a storm. For the author the prophet's sleep is the demonstration of lack of concern for the common good. To fall asleep in the hold of the ship is to register not simply dissatisfaction with God's plan but total rejection of it. Secondly, while the pagans are organizing a prayer service to placate the gods of the storm, the prophet of Israel remains hardened in his unrepentance. The pagans thereby become the model of prayer while the prophet is the example of religious apathy.

In his actions Jonah displays a remarkable inconsistency. He does not disparage these pagan mariners. However, he does disparage the Ninevites and not even a storm will free him from his entrenched theological position. His intransigency implies that the Lord should adopt a similar policy. In the face of the greatest compassion the Lord should hold fast to his resolve to balance the punishment of Nineveh against the record of gross sinfulness. Jonah would be the Lord's Director of Public Prosecutions, urging that the punishment fit the crime. In Jonah's ledger there is no room for Yahweh's freedom. For the prophet, to be Yahweh means to get control of one's emotions, resist leniency, and pull the plug on the hated Ninevites.

FROM REFUSAL
TO COMPLIANCE
1:17—3:3a.

The motifs in chap. 2 correspond to those in chap. 1, although the protagonists are here limited to the Lord and Jonah. In v.3 (but see 1:17) a crisis situation develops when the prophet experiences the threat of death. His response to this crisis takes the form of a prayer (v.2). Yahweh deigns to react positively to Jonah's prayer by delivering him from death (v.6). Finally Jonah acknowledges Yahweh's graciousness by cultic acts: sacrifices and vows (v.9). The structure, therefore, of this section matches that in 1:1-16 and suggests a carefully conceived plan.

The material may be divided as follows: (1) Jonah's new habitat (1:17); (2) the psalm (2:1-9); (3) compliance at last (2:10-3:3a).

JONAH'S NEW HABITAT
1:17.

>[17]And the Lord appointed a great fish to swallow up Jonah; and Jonah was in the belly of the fish three days and three nights.

In this carefully conceived plan the fish plays a key role, although not a central one. The author uses one of his favorite adjectives to describe the fish — it is "great." By so doing, the author does not impose on the reader the burden of research to determine the appropriate size of gullet and ultimately the exact species of fish, e.g., the sperm whale. The author's intent, rather, is to force the reader to recognize the fish as an instrument of God's freedom: "And the Lord *appointed.*" (See also 4:6-8.) While the fish is an element of exaggeration in the story, it fittingly symbolizes God's sovereign liberty — in this case to deliver (unlike Amos 9:3).

THE PSALM
2:1-9.

2 Then Jonah prayed to the Lord his God from the belly of the fish, ²saying,
"I called to the Lord, out of my distress,
  and he answered me;
out of the belly of Sheol I cried,
  and thou didst hear my voice.
³For thou didst cast me into the deep, into the heart
  of the seas;
  and the flood was round about me;
all thy waves and thy billows passed over me.
⁴Then I said, 'I am cast out from thy presence;
  how shall I again look upon thy holy temple?"
⁵The waters closed in over me, the deep was round
  about me;
  weeds were wrapped about my head
⁶at the roots of the mountains.
 I went down to the land
  whose bars closed upon me for ever;
  yet thou didst bring up my life from the Pit,
  O Lord my God.
⁷When my soul fainted within me
  I remembered the Lord;
and my prayer came to thee, into thy holy temple.
⁸Those who pay regard to vain idols
  forsake their true loyalty.

> ⁹But I with the voice of thanksgiving
>   will sacrifice to thee;
> what I have vowed I will pay.
>   Deliverance belongs to the Lord!"

The psalm of 2:2-9 is something of a contrast to the prose of the rest of the account. Many authors hold that it is not the work of the original author of Jonah but of a later redactor. Such authors point out that psalm praying does not suit the predicament of the prophet: the belly of the fish is not the locus for prayer. Moreover, they urge that prayer is not in keeping with Jonah's character. The Jonah of the psalm appears to be a man of faith, whereas the Jonah of the rest of the book is a violent individual diametrically opposed to God's will. Finally the vocabulary and style of the psalm are different from the prose sections.

Although the theory of a later redactor is still a common position, there is a move to consider the psalm the work of the original author in one way or another. The structure of the psalm corresponds to the structure of 1:1-16. Psalm praying in the belly of a great fish does relate to Jonah's personal predicament, as opposed to his concern for the fate of the Ninevites. Jonah thus emerges as a complicated character. He is a sincere believer but a violent believer. His view of Yahweh's ability to give determines his reactions in different situations.

The emphasis on death in the psalm blends in with the rest of the story. Moreover, the crisis situation, the response of those in crisis, Yahweh's reply, and the reaction of those delivered are the very essence of this intriguing story in all four chapters. It seems likely that the author of the story found this preexisting psalm and carefully worked it into his narrative. Such a procedure would account for the differences in vocabulary and style. The psalm is not, therefore, a later but happy adjunct to the account but an essential ingredient in the author's delineation of his audience. They are Jonah praying in the belly of a great fish.

The psalm may be classified as a declarative psalm of

praise by the individual (see also Pss 9; 18; 32; 34). Instead of focusing on praise of God's being and general activity (descriptive psalm of praise), it stresses praise of God's saving acts, here for an individual. (Verse 9 tends to become somewhat general, however.) In such a psalm the one rescued recounts how God intervened on his behalf and protests his determination to offer the proper sacrifices and fulfill his vows. The cultic association of this preexisting psalm, therefore, accounts for the switch between the second (vv.2b, 3, 4, 6b, 7b, 9a) and third (vv.2a, 7a, 8, 9b) persons. It also explains the sacrifices of v.9a.

At the same time, however, the author of Jonah has adapted the psalm to meet the needs of his story. Verse 3 describes the predicament of the psalmist as one of drowning. However, the drowning is clearly an image of the great danger threatening the original psalmist — whether that danger be death as resulting from sickness, enemies, etc. The author of Jonah, however, has interpreted the drowning literally. The Lord has made the pagan sailors his instruments in a possible drowning death. In this adaptation Jonah experiences the perils of the sea whereas the original psalmist encountered dangers from other quarters. As a result, the psalm serves the needs of the story. It is now read and prayed on a different level.

In view of Jonah's flight from the Lord's presence (1:3), it is interesting to note the emphasis on that presence in the psalm. Verse 4b is best translated: " 'nevertheless (in RSV "how") I shall look again upon thy holy temple.' " One need not assume that the author of Jonah had his principal character yearn for Yahweh's presence in a Palestinian sanctuary. The sanctuary or temple is the place where Yahweh hears the prayers of his people. According to v.7b the prayer arrived there and Yahweh deigned to reply to the petitioner's need.

There is irony in such a prayer. The prophet who flees now seeks the security of temple-oriented prayer. The one who flees *from* the Lord must flee *to* the Lord. The prayer reveals the humanity of the prophet stripped of its theological prejudices. When life (in v.7a " 'my soul' " means "my life" or "I") is threatened, both pagans and believers resort to the same solution, prayer to Yahweh. Although Jonah refused to cry out to the Lord during the storm (1:6), he now cries out in desperation because of personal distress (in v.2 of RSV " 'I called' "). The pagans and Jonah are odd bedfellows but a personal danger provokes a personal prayer. At the same time the author establishes his point: a genuine cry for help is efficacious, whether it stems from pagan sailors or a believing/disbelieving prophet.

Jonah has experienced Sheol or the nether world. In v.6 it is described as " 'the land' " and " 'the Pit.' " According to Amos 9:2; Job 26:6 Sheol is a region outside the earth but one which is accessible to the Lord. According to Hebrew cosmogony it was under the earth (Num 16:30) in the lower part of the cosmic ocean (Job 26:5) and Jonah 2:5 localizes it at the roots of the mountains. Verse 5 adds to this watery image by noting the presence of seaweed. A final image is that of a city with gates (v.6). In 1:17 the author states that the length of Jonah's sojourn in the belly of the fish/Sheol was three days and three nights. In ancient Near Eastern texts such a period corresponds to the length of time required for a journey between the upper and nether worlds.

It is not by accident that the author dwells on the subject of death. Prior to the second century B.C. there is no clear evidence of an afterlife. Sheol was the denial of life itself. Indeed, in Sheol one could not even praise God (Ps 6:6). In this listless state of inactivity one experienced radical separation from God. Jonah, therefore, reacts in typical Israelite fashion by striving to hold on to life at all costs. His prayer clearly shows that he regards death as a great evil. However, the subsequent events in Nineveh will completely alter the prophet's attitude towards death. At that point he will welcome death as a great relief because he prefers to perish with his warped theology than to live with a wider vision of God's liberty. The life of Nineveh demands the death of the prophet.

The conclusion of the psalm is another ironical touch.

Here Jonah sings: " 'Deliverance belongs to the Lord!' " Without any special claim on God's mercy Jonah experiences great compassion. It is a compassion which cannot be fitted into a theological equation. Yahweh chooses to deliver because Yahweh is Yahweh. In this concluding statement the prophet unequivocally announces what he will later deny to the Ninevites. It is one thing for Jonah to experience such deliverance, it is another for him to transfer that deliverance to the Ninevites. Though a pious believer, Jonah refuses to break free of the dehumanizing grip of a God made in his own image. By clinging to his narrow views of God's liberty, Jonah is guilty of idolatry — he has made a false image.

COMPLIANCE AT LAST
2:10—3:3a.

> ¹⁰And the Lord spoke to the fish, and it vomited out Jonah upon the dry land.
> 3   Then the word of the Lord came to Jonah the second time, saying, ²"Arise, go to Nineveh, that great city, and proclaim to it the message that I tell you." ³So Jonah arose and went to Nineveh, according to the word of the Lord.

At the end of chap. 2 the Lord conveniently arranges for the fish to regurgitate its human cargo on the Palestinian coast. God speaks a second time, repeating the command given in 1:2. The prophet is once again called upon to proclaim. In 2:1 Jonah did proclaim (" 'I called' ") but then it was a question of personal need. The reader is left with the question: how will the prophet react when it is a question of the communal need of Nineveh? The scene closes with a statement of material compliance, unlike chap. 1: "So Jonah arose and went to Nineveh, according to the word of the Lord." But have the experiences of chaps. 1 and 2 really wrought a change in the prophet's attitude?

FROM PROCLAMATION
TO REPENTANCE
TO COMPASSION
3:3b-10.

The structure of this section again involves the elements of crisis, response, and reaction. In v.4 a crisis situation, viz., destruction, confronts the city of Nineveh. In vv.5-8 the Ninevites respond to this crisis situation by a dramatic display of conversion and repentance. Given such a response, Yahweh reacts by having a change of heart and thus withdrawing his plan to destroy the city (v.10). As we will see, this structure will reappear in chap. 4 in the show-down between the Lord and Jonah.

This scene is also linked to 1:1-16. Once again the prophet (and the Lord) finds himself among pagans. Whereas it was previously the captain of the ship and his crew, it is now the king of Nineveh, its citizenry, and even its livestock. The reader is anxious to learn how the seemingly obedient prophet will react in this new pagan setting.

The material may be divided as follows: (1) proclamation (3:3b-4); (2) repentance (3:5-9); (3) compassion (3:10).

PROCLAMATION
3:3b-4.

Now Nineveh was an exceedingly great city, three days'

> journey in breadth. ⁴Jonah began to go into the city,
> going a day's journey. And he cried, "Yet forty days, and
> Nineveh shall be overthrown!"

The author begins his description of the city of Nineveh by describing it with his typical adjective "great," but qualifying it with "exceedingly" (literally: "great [even] for God"). Although no longer in existence, Nineveh would have been enormous in comparison with cities in Israel at the time. According to the author it was a three-day walk. Although the RSV interprets this in terms of breadth, it could conceivably refer to the circumference. Once again, however, the author has indulged in exaggeration in order to dramatize the Ninevite response to God's word. While a three-day walk would suggest something like fifty miles, the actual excavations of the site have disclosed an inner wall, seven and a half miles long, which enclosed an area of less than three square miles. According to the Assyrian annals a day's walk through the Nineveh of Sennacherib's time (704-681 B.C.) would have taken Jonah well beyond the center of the city. Exaggeration, however, in the service of the word of God allows for significant discrepancies.

The message of the prophet is terse enough: in English eight words, in Hebrew five. In the light of Jonah's theological convictions the reader may legitimately wonder if the prophet himself has not attached the timetable to the message. The verb "to overthrow" certainly evokes the destruction of the cities of Sodom and Gomorrah in Gen 19:21, 25, 29. However, the verb is also ambiguous enough to mean a change of person or of heart, as in the case of Saul in 1 Sam 10:6, 9. While the prophet would have intended the meaning of Gen 19, the author may be suggesting the sense of 1 Sam 10.

Although Jonah has not really changed, the author uses his halfhearted effort to make some telling theological points. The God of Israel is a God of hope. Jonah thereby becomes God's chosen, if reluctant and unconvinced, instrument to offer others the possibility of reconciliation.

God would yet speak to those living on the brink of disaster. At the same time, while Yahweh's freedom remains intact, a response is required. The God of Israel respects the liberty of the Ninevites by calling for a change of heart. While Yahweh remains Yahweh, humans also remain humans —free.

REPENTANCE
3:5-9.

> ⁵And the people of Nineveh believed God; they proclaimed a fast, and put on sackcloth, from the greatest of them to the least of them.
> ⁶Then tidings reached the king of Nineveh, and he arose from his throne, removed his robe, and covered himself with sackcloth, and sat in ashes. ⁷And he made proclamation and published through Nineveh, "By the decree of the king and his nobles: Let neither man nor beast, herd nor flock, taste anything; let them not feed, or drink water, ⁸but let man and beast be covered with sackcloth, and let them cry mightily to God; yea, let every one turn from his evil way and from the violence which is in his hands. ⁹Who knows, God may yet repent and turn from his fierce anger, so that we perish not?"

In v.5 the unexpected — for Jonah — the impossible takes place. Even though the prophet has covered only one third of the city, a massive conversion reaction develops which subsequently engulfs the entire populace. The terse message of destruction has produced total conversion. It is significant that the Ninevites recognize the presence of God in the message of the prophet. Upon hearing the words of Jonah, the Ninevites believe in God. They have thereby opened themselves up to the possibility of a completely new life. They have chosen to base themselves on and be rooted in the God of Israel.

Verses 6-8 flesh out this total acceptance of Yahweh. Even the hated king of Nineveh (left unnamed by the author), the greatest political figure in the ancient Near East of the eighth century B.C., succumbs to the power of the word. Although in Persia animals were decked out in mourning garb (see Jdt 4:10), the author employs this detail to underline the totality of the conversion: it includes even the animal world. Like the sailors in 1:14, the Ninevites cry out mightily to the Lord (in v.5 the same verb is used — in RSV "they proclaimed a fast"). The Ninevites thus become models of conversion for the author's audience.

One is reminded of Joel 1-2 where everyone in a threatened Jerusalem responds to the call for penance — a response which averts God's judgment (Joel 2:18-19). The pagans of Jonah 3 exhibit the same qualities as the Jerusalemites of Joel 1-2. To think that all this happened in Nineveh because Jonah "cried" (v.4)!

COMPASSION
3:10.

> [10]When God saw what they did, how they turned from their evil way, God repented of the evil which he had said he would do to them; and he did not do it.

The RSV translates God's reaction to the Ninevite change of heart as "repent" (vv.9, 10). The Hebrew root, however, has the nuance of compassion. In v.9 the king suggests that perhaps God may once again show compassion. In v.10 the author relates that God was sorry for the evil he had threatened. Such compassion is an exercise of the Lord's sovereignty. No one has the right to set up parameters for the exercise of his sovereignty. To be God is to have the right to give, especially in the absence of any claims.

While the proper response of the Ninevites is a requirement for deliverance, there is no automatic relationship between that response and deliverance. Ultimately deliverance is rooted in the Lord's sovereign freedom. Verse 9 expresses this when the king reveals his insight into God's radical ability to give — an insight which is still lacking in the Israelite prophet.

The author clearly subscribes to the power of the word. While humans remain free to accept or reject that word, it still retains an inherent ability to provoke a decision. Not even the less than enthusiastic proclamation of Jonah can offset the efficacy of the word. Perhaps the author leaves the audience with questions: what would have been the effect of Jonah's proclamation, if he wholeheartedly endorsed it?

JONAH'S ANGER AND GOD'S COMPASSION 4:1-11.

The structure of chap. 4 corresponds to 3:3b-10. A crisis situation develops for Jonah since Nineveh's destruction seems to have been averted (this is the apparent background of v.1). Jonah responds to this crisis by anger, attacks on God, and the desire to die (vv.1-3). Yahweh finally reacts to Jonah. By dint of dialog and action Yahweh attempts to bring about a change of heart in Jonah relative to the salvation of Nineveh (vv.4, 6-11).

Only the Lord and Jonah occupy the stage in chap. 4. All the previous action has been building towards this climax. The experiences on the high seas, in Sheol, and in Nineveh are the precedents which color the exchange between the Lord and the prophet. Only after such scenes is the author ready to reveal the "real" Jonah.

The material may be divided as follows: (1) Jonah's reaction and God's reply (4:1-4); (2) the gourd plant (4:5-9); (3) a theology of gift (4:10-11).

JONAH'S REACTION AND GOD'S REPLY 4:1-4.

4 But it displeased Jonah exceedingly, and he was

angry. ²And he prayed to the Lord and said, "I pray thee, Lord, is not this what I said when I was yet in my country? That is why I made haste to flee to Tarshish; for I knew that thou art a gracious God and merciful, slow to anger, and abounding in steadfast love, and repentest of evil. ³Therefore now, O Lord, take my life from me, I beseech thee, for it is better for me to die than to live." ⁴And the Lord said, "Do you do well to be angry?"

Anger adequately describes Jonah's reaction. The author employs the verb "to be angry" (literally: "to be hot") in vv.1, 4, 9 (2x). Verse 1 begins by noting that Jonah was furious. Literally: "And it was evil to Jonah, a great evil." This contrasts with the response of the Ninevites who turned from their evil way (see 3:8, 10). Confronted by the actions of Nineveh, the *great* city, the prophet can demonstrate only a *great* evil or fury. Jonah's reaction also contrasts with the Lord who was sorry for his threatened evil (3:10) and so turned away from his fierce anger (3:9). While the Lord is slow to anger (v.2), the prophet is all too quick. Both the Lord and the Ninevites are the exact opposite of the prophet.

The reader now learns that the flight to Tarshish was not Jonah's first contact with the Lord over the mission to the Ninevites. Verse 2 refers to a previous encounter in which the prophet explained to the Lord the possible dire consequences of such a mission. The deliverance of Nineveh was in the back of the prophet's mind all the time. The "real" Jonah is now standing up. What Jonah feared all along has become a reality. The nightmare of the city's salvation now haunts him.

Jonah's prayer in vv.2-3 is hardly a model of proper communing with the Lord, although it is a good example of honesty. The prophet recites the old confession that Yahweh is a gracious and merciful God (see Exod 34:6; Num 14:18-19). He even adds what 3:9-10 has already demonstrated, viz., that the Lord is compassionate. While this may apply to Yahweh's dealings with Israel, Jonah cannot possibly see its application in Yahweh's dealings with the worst of the pagan world, Nineveh.

The prayer is Jonah's ego trip. Nine times in vv.2-3 (ten times in the English text) the prophet uses "I," "my," or "me." The prophet had always taken good care of himself and his own theology. Now the Lord's compassion for Nineveh is an assault on his ego. To accept the deliverance of Nineveh is to infer that his actions had been egotistical right from the start. His ego prevents him from rejoicing in the happiness of others. Whereas the captain, sailors, king, and Ninevites sought for life in the face of death, Jonah now seeks death in the face of life. His request for death recalls Elijah's similar request in 1 Kgs 19:4. The difference, however, is that Elijah was threatened by real danger in the form of Queen Jezebel, whereas Jonah is threatened by no danger except the product of his warped theological system. Jonah cannot rejoice with those who rejoice.

Jonah's prayer is also linked to the psalm in 2:2-9. Both prayers relate previous experiences of discomfort and distress. Both reflect Yahweh's deliverance. In 2:9 Jonah exclaims that deliverance belongs to the Lord; in 4:2-3 Jonah concludes that the deliverance of the Ninevites is in keeping with the Lord's compassionate nature. Both betray Jonah's response to God's saving action. In 2:9 Jonah promises to offer the sacrifices and fulfill the vows appropriate for the occasion. In 4:2-3 the prophet evinces great rage and asks to die. When it is a question of his personal safety, Jonah breaks out into paroxyms of gratitude. When it is a question of the safety of others, the prophet wallows in self-pity.

The Lord's question in v.4 revolves around deliverance. The Lord asks if the prophet is right in being angry. This apparently harmless question reveals a more subtle attack on God's freedom. In Jonah's judgment his anger was the only proper response to Yahweh's reckless endangering of sound theology. Although the prophet had recited the confession whereby the Lord is slow to anger, he protests that Yahweh has overstepped, not only the bounds of propriety, but even the limits of his own nature. It is only too clear to the prophet that Yahweh refuses to be angry. If Yahweh has thus abdicated his own right to judge, then Jonah will exercise that prerogative for him. The Jonah computer is programmed to demand retribution because of Nineveh's heinousness. Not to demand such retribution is to yield to weakness and softness. The God made in Jonah's image can never be so weak or soft.

THE GOURD PLANT
4:5-9.

> 5Then Jonah went out of the city and sat to the east of the city, and made a booth for himself there. He sat under it in the shade, till he should see what would become of the city.
> 6And the Lord God appointed a plant, and made it come up over Jonah, that it might be a shade over his head, to save him from his discomfort. So Jonah was exceedingly glad because of the plant. 7But when dawn came up the next day, God appointed a worm which attacked the plant, so that it withered. 8When the sun rose, God appointed a sultry east wind, and the sun beat upon the head of Jonah so that he was faint; and he asked that he might die, and said, "It is better for me to die than to live." 9But God said to Jonah, "Do you do well to be angry for the plant?" And he said, "I do well to be angry, angry enough to die."

Jonah will not yield. There is still the glimmer of hope that Nineveh will reap its harvest of annihilation. Consequently the prophet moves farther east and erects a makeshift hut to provide shade from the sun. (The hut is open at the back or eastern side [see v.8].) Here Jonah positions himself to await the outcome. It is clear that the Lord's question in v.4 only irritated him. Perhaps the Lord will be consistent. If so, he will have a perfect view of the city when the great city gets the reward for its great evil.

The Lord will not yield. Instead of destroying the city, the

Lord has decided to destroy Jonah's flimsy theology. The only fitting way to accomplish the task is once again a demonstration of the Lord's freedom. The author captures this exercise of freedom by using the verb "to appoint" three times (see also 1:17). In v.6 the Lord *appoints* a gourd plant, i.e., a plant with wide leaves belonging to the cucumber or castor-bean species. Its purpose is to provide shade and thus save Jonah from his *evil* (in RSV "discomfort"). Jonah's reaction is great joy, the very opposite of the great evil in v.1. In v.7 the Lord *appoints* a worm to attack the plant at dawn and thus undo the sudden and miraculous growth. In v.8 the Lord *appoints* a sultry east wind which was complicated by the hot sun pouring through the opening in the hut. At this point the prophet reiterates his wish to die.

The author's exaggeration is to his advantage. He matches the sudden conversion of Nineveh with the sudden growth and demise of the plant. In turn, the fate of the plant reflects the egocentric stance of the prophet. He experiences great joy because the plant delivers him from the searing sun. Yet he experiences great anger because Yahweh delivers Nineveh from its due punishment. He experiences great anger because Yahweh destroys the plant. Yet he would experience great joy, if Yahweh would only destroy Nineveh.

Not to be outdone, Yahweh resumes his questioning in v.9. The Lord asks if Jonah really has a right to be angry about the destruction of the plant. The question indicates a larger problem area. It includes not just Nineveh but also Israel as represented in the person of the prophet. Jonah's anger argues in favor of a line of demarcation whereby Nineveh and Israel would be clearly distinguished. The Lord's questioning implies that Jonah has no right to foist his preconceived notions of construction/destruction on the operations of God's freedom.

A THEOLOGY OF GIFT
4:10-11.

> ¹⁰And the Lord said, "You pity the plant, for which you did not labor, nor did you make it grow, which came into being in a night, and perished in a night. ¹¹And should not I pity Nineveh, that great city, in which there are more than a hundred and twenty thousand persons who do not know their right hand from their left, and also much cattle?"

In v.10 the argument moves into the area of a theology of gift. The plant cost the prophet no labor at all. It was a twenty-four hour creation. Its demise was as sudden as its growth, so that the prophet had no chance to get attached to it. Yet Jonah would place the plant on the same level as the people of Nineveh! In terms of justice the prophet cannot muster any reasons to establish his right to the plant and therefore legitimate his grievance at its demise. The plant is the sacrament of God's radical ability to give. To pervert the plant into a legal precedent is to deny God the right to be a giver of gifts apart from any legal claims.

The Lord's sovereignty in giving becomes even clearer in v.11. The verb "to pity" (see also v.10) is often used in contexts of sovereign power and jurisdiction. In Ps 72 [71]:13 and Jer 21:7 such compassion is appropriate or inappropriate for a king. In Deut 19:13, 21 and 25:12 this compassion is unbecoming a representative of the people. In showing compassion for the Ninevites Yahweh opts to exercise his royal prerogatives, especially his freedom. On the other hand, Jonah has no basis or right to exercise this pity in favor of the plant. Against such a background v.11 may be rendered: " 'And may I not pity . . .?' " rather than the RSV " 'And should not I pity?' " (see Mt 20:15).

The contrast between Jonah's plant and Yahweh's Nineveh also emerges in v.11. Yahweh opposes the population of the city of Nineveh to Jonah's plant. Although some authors tend to interpret the 120,000 as children, the text ("persons") and the context speak in favor of understanding the adult population as children. The fact that the inhabitants of the city are unable to make their own judgments is all the more reason why Nineveh should be preferred to the plant.

The book concludes with a question. It is, however, a challenge directed to ongoing generations of believers as well. It is the challenge either to identify with the neat "quid pro quo" theology of Jonah or to opt for a non-manipulative view of God's freedom. More radically, perhaps, it is the challenge to adopt Jonah's view of people as things or to accept Yahweh's understanding of people as people. To preserve God's reputation as the giver of gifts and hence the God of surprises is as timely as ever.

The Book of Ruth

CONTENTS

INTRODUCTION TO
THE BOOK OF RUTH

The Appeal of the Book

Ruth deals with seemingly ordinary, everyday events. There is nothing similar to the pogrom of Ahasuerus in Esther, the attack of Holofernes in Judith, the wonder drugs and exorcisms in Tobit, or the miraculous conversions in Jonah. Ruth is a study in the apparently trivial occurrences of a family: famine, bereavement, gleaning, feasting at the threshing floor, the search for a husband, the desire for a family, the birth of a child. Ruth creates the impression of being mundane and secular but it is only an impression.

Ruth is the story of the hidden God of Israel. Unlike Hebrew Esther, Ruth does mention God's name and intervention. But human protagonists predominate. The beauty of the book is that God is present whenever humans are truly concerned about the needs and problems of fellow humans. God acts responsibly because humans act responsibly. The seemingly profane events are the raw material for covenant loyalty and support. The ordinary happenings are thereby transformed into extraordinary occasions for demonstrating the presence of the seemingly aloof God of Israel.

Blessings, invocations, and lamentations abound in the book. They are addressed to Yahweh but humans become the channels of God's response. To utter a blessing is in effect to be willing to provide help for the destitute. To cry out in lament is to expect God's aid in the generous giving of fellow Israelites. Peace becomes a reality only because others will provoke the setting of peace. The God of Israel is in evidence because Israel is in evidence.

The Book of Ruth is a study in divine providence. The complexities of ordinary human existence call for a divine resolution. The hungry must be fed, the widow must be provided for, property must be kept in the family. The God of Israel cares for the people exposed to such dangers. He cares by prompting others to react to human plight and see such plight as a faith opportunity. Yahweh provides because others provide.

The Book of Ruth is a story of human liberation. In a male-dominated society Naomi and Ruth must determine their own survival without the benefit of husbands. The two widows initiate the actions. Even when Boaz intervenes, he is responding to their initiatives. In a man's world these two women are center stage. They are the catalysts for divine intervention. They shock, they provoke, they intimidate. Ruth is the story of two women in reaction to the limitations of patriarchal society. It is the abiding story of humans who yearn to contribute to the community in the face of all obstacles. It is a story of faith which continues to challenge the faith community.

The Setting of the Book

The story opens during the time of the Judges, a period which lasted about two centuries (cir. 1200-1025 B.C.). During this time there was no national unity, although some of the Israelite tribes would band together periodically to ward off a common enemy. Israel's awareness at this time was its faith awareness, i.e., the experience of the Exodus which the participating tribes had brought into the Promised Land. A united political awareness was yet to come.

The story actually concludes in 4:17 with the announcement of the birth of Obed, the grandfather of King David.

This note involves an historical transition. Towards the end of the eleventh century B.C. Israel realized that its survival demanded the establishment of a monarchy. The local tribal leaders were no longer capable of defending their land and their people. The Book of Ruth, therefore, has its setting in such a time of transition. The very mention of the name of David warns the reader that a new order, a new atmosphere was developing at this time.

The author writes an eminently plausible story. The lack of rain in Judah causes a famine which necessitates the departure of Elimelech's family to a more fertile area in Moab. The customs of levirate marriage and redemption, besides contributing to the atmosphere of the story, are credible institutions. The agricultural life with its seasons of growing and harvesting is not pure fantasy. The city life itself with the threshing floor and the gatherings at the city gate is not only vivid but also believable. The author has not contrived events comparable to those in Esther, Judith, Tobit, and Jonah. He has provided a plausible setting in which the seemingly implausible actions of a concerned God may take place.

Origins and Literary Form

Like the Book of Jonah, the Book of Ruth is a short story. Yet Ruth differs significantly from Jonah. Unlike Jonah, Ruth is a plausible story. It does not introduce extraordinary or miraculous events. Unlike Jonah, Ruth focuses on rather typical and ordinary happenings. The fish, the conversion, and the plant of the Book of Jonah give way to the barley harvest, the threshing floor, and the sale of property of the Book of Ruth. While both Jonah and Ruth entertain and instruct, they do so in diametrically opposed ways.

Ruth is an historical short story. While it does not depend on historicity, Ruth provides plausibility. It combines brevity with several interconnected episodes, but in a setting where the reader is prone to accept the realism of the characters. Unlike Jonah, Ruth invites the reader to identify with the concrete needs, the human sentiments, and the appealing situations of the characters. Ruth is a piece of life, not a pilot project in the unraveling of God's providence.

At the same time Ruth, while fictional, may rely on an old, authentic tradition. According to 4:17 Ruth the Moabitess is the great-grandmother of David. It is hard to imagine that this detail was contrived at a later date when the figure of David was so exalted. According to 1 Sam 22:3 David, who was being pursued by Saul, sought the aid of the king of Moab for his parents. The Moabite king thereupon provided protection during the time of Saul's persecution. Although this detail should not be pressed, it does suggest ancestral ties to Moab, ties which offer a dimension of plausibility to the short story.

The growth of the story is difficult to see. Some authors prefer an old poetic tale which was subsequently converted into a prose account. Others would emphasize a charming story about fidelity and love which was later brought into harmony with Israelite legal practices. While the language in Ruth is rhythmical, particularly in the speeches, the old poetic tale is not sufficiently established. Although details were probably already present in oral tradition, the Book of Ruth appears to be a unique literary creation. It is the product of a new era in the history of Israel.

As a short story, Ruth is basically a comedy. It begins with the despair of two widows. The death of husbands and the absence of children are formidable obstacles to their survival. The book witnesses, however, to their bold, courageous efforts to offset their plight. The story concludes on a happy note, viz., the birth of a child. Though Naomi is still a widow, she is now a grandmother. As for Ruth, she is not only a wife and a mother but also the great-grandmother of King David. Despair has yielded to hope and hope has given way to actual blessing. "All's well that ends well."

The Author's Purpose

The intent of the original author is not to be judged by the position of Ruth in the canon. In the Hebrew Bible it is found in the third division or Writings. Like Esther, it is one of the scrolls — the festal reading for Pentecost or Weeks. (This period of "fifty" days includes the beginning of the barley harvest and the end of the wheat harvest.) In the Greek and Latin translations Ruth is found after Judges and before First Samuel. It is thus a transitional piece which prepares for the activity of King David.

A once common view was that Ruth was written to protest the prohibition of mixed marriages in the postexilic period, a prohibition generally linked with the names of Ezra and Nehemiah (cir. 450-400 B.C.). Thus, if David's great-grandmother was a Moabitess, mixed marriages should not be summarily forbidden. Other authors see the purpose as an effort to underline the devotion of a daughter-in-law to her mother-in-law. Finally, still others would consider the story an example of the practice of levirate marriage.

The heavily covenantal language of the book suggests another approach. The mutual support which the book recommends is a concrete example of living out the implications of covenant. The story is the story of the hidden God of Israel who becomes manifest when his people meet the needs and concerns of fellow Israelites. While limiting itself to a given historical situation, the book endorses covenantal love in all situations. When Israel raises the question about the meaning and practice of covenant, she need only consider the interaction of Naomi and Ruth, the concern of Boaz, and the somewhat negative stance of the unnamed redeemer.

While Ruth emphasizes covenant, it does not accept a mechanical doctrine of reward and punishment after the manner of the Book of Deuteronomy. The Deuteronomic theology of Tobit is necessarily absent from Ruth. In Ruth God does not send angels who will provide rewards. In Ruth

God provokes humans to find their own reward in serving others.

Time of Composition

Although Ruth was long considered a postexilic work, recent commentators now rally to a preexilic date. The legal practices in Ruth (e.g., levirate marriage and redemption), while they differ from those contained in Leviticus and Deuteronomy, need not be late. They can simply reflect earlier practices which were further developed and then codified. The supposed universalism of Ruth, viz., opposition to the prohibition of mixed marriages, simply begs the question. The language, once thought to be late, now offers evidence of being early. As for the genealogy in 4:18-22, it is commonly agreed that this is the work of a later hand.

On the positive side, Ruth may be compared with such works as the Succession Narrative (2 Sam 9-20; 1 Kgs 1-2) and Joseph Story (Gen 37-50 [in general]). Both of these works are products of Israel's period of enlightenment, i.e., a period which begins around the middle of the tenth century B.C. (Most of the Joseph Story is to be assigned to the Yahwist of the late tenth century B.C.) In these works God is in charge, because humans are in charge. God's presence is no longer bound up with local shrines or charismatic leaders (the Judges). God's presence is now linked to the bold decisions of humans, as they seek to address the needs of their world in a human way. The faults and foibles of the principal characters are not whitewashed. The God of Israel works in and through human weakness.

It is difficult to pinpoint the date of composition of Ruth. However, a time somewhere between the tenth and eighth centuries B.C. does not seem unreasonable. Ruth thereby disappears from the "reaction" literature of the postexilic period. It is a product of the preexilic period which challenges all subsequent periods.

DEPARTURE AND RETURN
1:1-22.

The first few verses set the stage for the entire story by introducing the principal characters and their common predicament. The main part of the chapter then describes the plight of the women and their efforts to avert catastrophe. The material may be divided as follows: (1) catastrophe (1:1-5); (2) coping with catastrophe (1:6-22).

CATASTROPHE
1:1-5.

1 In the days when the judges ruled there was a famine in the land, and a certain man of Bethlehem in Judah went to sojourn in the country of Moab, he and his wife and his two sons. ²The name of the man was Elimelech and the name of his wife Naomi, and the names of his two sons were Mahlon and Chilion; they were Ephrathites from Bethlehem in Judah. They went into the country of Moab and remained there. ³But Elimelech, the husband of Naomi, died, and she was left with her two sons. ⁴These

took Moabite wives; the name of the one was Orpah and
the name of the other Ruth. They lived there about ten
years; [5]and both Mahlon and Chilion died, so that the
woman was bereft of her two sons and her husband.

The names of the three men and Naomi stress the desper-
ateness of the situation. "Elimelech" means: "My God is
king." Yet his death raises the question whether or not
Yahweh is really in control. While the etymology of the
sons' names can be interpreted differently, the popular
meaning must have been telling for the audience. "Chilion"
suggests "destruction" while "Mahlon" conjures up "dis-
ease." Finally, Naomi's name focuses on the providence of
God. Her name is probably a shortened nickname meaning:
"(My) pleasantness (is God)." Yet, as v.20 indicates, God
has proved to be bitterness, not pleasantness to Naomi.

The ten-year period can refer to the entire time of the
sojourn in Moab. But within the context of the whole story
it probably refers to the childless marriages. This is by way
of contrast with 4:13 where Ruth conceives immediately.
During this time Naomi has reached menopause (v.11). The
possibility of a family is bleak indeed.

Tragedy follows upon tragedy. Elimelech's death is followed by that of his two sons. The three women are now
childless widows and thereby deprived of identity as wives
and mothers. As a result, the security afforded by the male
society has vanished. It is interesting to note that the author
speaks of "his sons" in v.2 but of "her sons" in v.3, i.e., after
the death of Elimelech. The desperate situation calls for
equally desperate action.

COPING WITH CATASTROPHE
1:6-22.

[6]Then she started with her daughters-in-law to return
from the country of Moab, for she had heard in the
country of Moab that the Lord had visited his people and
given them food. [7]So she set out from the place where she

was, with her two daughters-in-law, and they went on the way to return to the land of Judah. ⁸But Naomi said to her two daughters-in-law, "Go, return each of you to her mother's house. May the Lord deal kindly with you, as you have dealt with the dead and with me. ⁹The Lord grant that you may find a home, each of you in the house of her husband!" Then she kissed them, and they lifted up their voices and wept. ¹⁰And they said to her, "No, we will return with you to your people." ¹¹But Naomi said, "Turn back, my daughters, why will you go with me? Have I yet sons in my womb that they may become your husbands? ¹²Turn back, my daughters, go your way, for I am too old to have a husband. If I should say I have hope, even if I should have a husband this night and should bear sons, ¹³would you therefore wait till they were grown? Would you therefore refrain from marrying? No, my daughters, for it is exceedingly bitter to me for your sake that the hand of the Lord has gone forth against me." ¹⁴Then they lifted up their voices and wept again; and Orpah kissed her mother-in-law, but Ruth clung to her.

¹⁵And she said, "See, your sister-in-law has gone back to her people and to her gods; return after your sister-in-law." ¹⁶But Ruth said, "Entreat me not to leave you or to return from following you; for where you go I will go, and where you lodge I will lodge; your people shall be my people, and your God my God; ¹⁷where you die I will die, and there will I be buried. May the Lord do so to me and more also if even death parts me from you." ¹⁸And when Naomi saw that she was determined to go with her, she said no more.

¹⁹So the two of them went on until they came to Bethlehem. And when they came to Bethlehem, the whole town was stirred because of them; and the women said, "Is this Naomi?" ²⁰She said to them, "Do not call me Naomi, call me Mara, for the Almighty has dealt very bitterly with me. ²¹I went away full, and the Lord has brought me back empty. Why call me Naomi, when the Lord has afflicted me and the Almighty has brought calamity upon me?"

²²So Naomi returned, and Ruth the Moabitess her daughter-in-law with her, who returned from the country of Moab. And they came to Bethlehem at the beginning of barley harvest.

The key verb in vv.6-22 is "to return." It appears no less than twelve times in the Hebrew text. It is not by chance that the author stresses this particular verb. The decision to return is ultimately the decision to cope with reality. It also indicates the difference in the two daughters-in-law: Orpah returns to her people whereas Ruth turns to Naomi's people. The return is also a trek in the direction of fullness. In v.21 Naomi laments that Shaddai has caused her to return empty. But, as the story unfolds, the emptiness of Moab gives way to the plenitude of Bethlehem.

With v.6 it is clear that the women are now in charge. Up to this verse Naomi was always identified in terms of her husband and children. Now for the first time she is the subject of a sentence and hence the initiator of a plan of action. In the opening verses the men played the key roles. Thus, in patriarchal style Elimelech led the family to the land of sojourn. But now Naomi assumes the leadership role. If men determined the past, then the women will plot out the future. Death has overtaken the men, the only possibility for life now lies with the women. Naomi, Ruth, and Orpah are now center stage.

Verses 8-9 offer the first example of covenant loyalty. Naomi prays that the Lord may do *hesed* (" 'deal kindly' ") to both Ruth and Orpah. This Hebrew term contains many nuances which we can perhaps compress into the translation "covenant loyalty." Naomi does not base her prayer on God's covenant loyalty, since from all appearances the Lord has refused to be involved. The basis for Yahweh's loving concern is the demonstration of such concern on the part of the two women towards the dead males. Because these humans have been loyal to fellow humans, then it is to be hoped that the Lord will be loyal to them in turn.

It is noteworthy that the covenant loyalty in question is not bound up with kings, temples, or extraordinary events. It is the covenant loyalty of everyday life whereby people reaffirm their pledged commitment to each other. Yet the prolonged demonstration of such "ordinary" loyalty is an extraordinary happening. It is rooted in God and makes

God present to the world.

Prayer is one of the key devices by which the author establishes a not-chance-but-providence theology. Prayer challenges other humans to assume their role of responsibility. It is, therefore, not by accident that Ruth finds a husband. The devout wish for a home in v.9 becomes more of a reality in 3:1 where Naomi, after hearing of Boaz's generosity, assures her daughter-in-law that she will find a home indeed.

Verses 10-13 reveal an urging, lamenting, intimating Naomi. Though deprived of her own identity, Naomi urges her daughters-in-law to return home. Although her own situation is more precarious, still Naomi looks to the interests of Ruth and Orpah. There is yet hope that they will find husbands and raise a family, thus regaining their identity.

Lamenting follows upon urging. Naomi has reached menopause. She laments that the Lord has turned against her and thereby eliminated all possible avenues of regaining her identity. Yet at the same time the author has Naomi intimate that the finding of a husband, at least for Ruth, will resolve her own bitterness and lack of identity. The levirate marriage can perhaps be the answer to the pressing problem.

Verses 14-18 compare the characters of the two daughters-in-law. Both choose their own future. In the case of Orpah her decision to return home is in agreement with Naomi's urging. But in the case of Ruth her decision to go to Judah is in disagreement with Naomi's urging. From a pragmatic point of view Orpah's determination alone makes sense. By returning home, she has the chance to begin anew. While Orpah chooses to be disassociated from her mother-in-law, Ruth chooses to be united with her. The author captures this disassociation in the kissing episode. Only Orpah returns Naomi's kiss (v.14).

Ruth's words and actions express covenant. In v.16 Ruth asks Naomi to desist from urging her daughter-in-law to leave. In v.14 she clings to her mother-in-law. In the Yahwist's account of marriage in Gen 2:24, which has a covenantal setting, a man *leaves* his parents and *clings* to his wife. In the covenant expression par excellence, the Book of Deuteronomy, Moses urges Israel to *cling* to the Lord (see Deut 10:20, 11:22, 13:4). Ruth persists in her expression of covenant loyalty by accepting Naomi's people and God as her people and God. In v.17 she also accepts Israelite burial customs and goes so far as to take a solemn oath that not even death will separate her from Naomi. Without benefit of a formal conversion ceremony Ruth has pledged her loyalty to the God of Israel. In effect, she promises to continue to live out the covenant loyalty she has thus far demonstrated. One must conclude that, while Orpah is indeed good, Ruth is far better. Covenant has become enfleshed in the resoluteness of this woman's indomitable spirit.

Verses 19-22 add to the anguish expressed in v.13. Naomi is an excellent example of Israel's awareness that one can complain to God, attack God, even insult God, but never dare to ignore God. By asking the women of Bethlehem to change her name from Naomi ("pleasantness") to Mara ("bitter"), she implicitly initiates a court case against Shaddai ("Almighty"). Her charge is that Yahweh has been unfaithful to the terms of the covenant. Naomi the full is now Naomi the empty. The RSV footnote for v.21 ("testified against") is more in keeping with Naomi's charge. Against the background of Exod 20:16 and Deut 5:20 she implies that Yahweh has played the part of a false witness. She adds, moreover, that Shaddai has meted out unjust punishment against her. The reader wonders how the Lord will respond to Naomi's charges.

Naomi's charges are followed by the author's remark that the two women returned to Bethlehem at the beginning of the barley harvest. The remark is innocent enough. But in view of the whole story the mention of the barley harvest is the beginning of Yahweh's response to Naomi's charges. For the author it is not chance, but providence which is at work. Because of the barley harvest Ruth will find herself gleaning in Boaz's fields. The scene will provoke another demonstration of covenant loyalty.

GLEANING
2:1-23.

Chapter two begins with the mention of Ruth's intention to go gleaning as well as the mention of a kinsman, viz., Boaz. The bulk of the chapter focuses on Ruth's gleaning in Boaz's field and their subsequent meeting. Next the author has Ruth return from the gleaning and converse with Naomi about the day's events. In a final note the author shows Ruth continuing to glean in Boaz's field.

The material may be divided as follows: (1) the resolve to go gleaning (2:1-2); (2) gleaning in Boaz's field (2:3-17); (3) Ruth's return and continued gleaning (2:18-23).

THE RESOLVE TO GO GLEANING
2:1-2.

> **2** Now Naomi had a kinsman of her husband's, a man of wealth, of the family of Elimelech, whose name was Boaz. ²And Ruth the Moabitess said to Naomi, "Let me go to the field, and glean among the ears of grain after him in whose sight I shall find favor." And she said to her, "Go, my daughter."

Verse 1 must be seen as at least a partial answer to Naomi's plight. The verse mentions three facts, all of which contribute to the denouement of chap. 4. First of all, Naomi has a kinsman. The word has a covenantal ring to it since the range of the verb "to know" includes covenantal responsibility. In fact, "covenant partner" may be a more accurate rendering than "kinsman" (see Pss 31 [30]:11; 55 [54]:13). With regard to Yahweh, to know him is to recognize him as sovereign and thus be willing to carry out the implications of covenant (see Hos 2:20; 4:1; 6:3, 6).

Secondly, the person in question is a man of substance. The Hebrew certainly covers the RSV translation ("wealth") but implies value and reputation as well (see Judg 6:12; 1 Kgs 11:28). In 3:11 Boaz will state that Ruth is also a person of worth and esteem.

Thirdly, the covenant partner is from Elimelech's family. The combination of covenant partner and family relationship suggests that Ruth's predicament can yet be solved through the levirate marriage. Cleverly the author withholds the name of Boaz until the end of the verse. By so doing, he arouses the reader's interest and creates an atmosphere of suspense.

GLEANING IN BOAZ'S FIELD
2:3-17.

> [3]So she set forth and went and gleaned in the field after the reapers; and she happened to come to the part of the field belonging to Boaz, who was of the family of Elimelech. [4]And behold, Boaz came from Bethlehem; and he said to the reapers, "The Lord be with you!" And they answered, "The Lord bless you." [5]Then Boaz said to his servant who was in charge of the reapers, "Whose maiden is this?" [6]And the servant who was in charge of the reapers answered, "It is the Moabite maiden, who came back with Naomi from the country of Moab. [7]She said, 'Pray, let me glean and gather among the sheaves after the reapers.' So she came, and she has continued from early morning until now, without resting even for a moment."
> [8]Then Boaz said to Ruth, "Now, listen, my daughter, do not go to glean in another field or leave this one, but

keep close to my maidens. 9Let your eyes be upon the field which they are reaping, and go after them. Have I not charged the young men not to molest you? And when you are thirsty, go to the vessels and drink what the young men have drawn." 10Then she fell on her face, bowing to the ground, and said to him, "Why have I found favor in your eyes, that you should take notice to me, when I am a foreigner?" 11But Boaz answered her, "All that you have done for your mother-in-law since the death of your husband has been fully told me, and how you left your father and mother and your native land and came to a people that you did not know before. 12The Lord recompense you for what you have done, and a full reward be given you by the Lord, the God of Israel, under whose wings you have come to take refuge!" 13Then she said, "You are most gracious to me, my lord, for you have comforted me and spoken kindly to your maidservant, though I am not one of your maidservants."

14And at mealtime Boaz said to her, "Come here, and eat some bread, and dip your morsel in the wine." So she sat beside the reapers, and he passed to her parched grain; and she ate until she was satisfied, and she had some left over. 15When she rose to glean, Boaz instructed his young men, saying, "Let her glean even among the sheaves, and do not reproach her. 16And also pull out some from the bundles for her, and leave it for her to glean, and do not rebuke her."

17So she gleaned in the field until evening; then she beat out what she had gleaned, and it was about an ephah of barley.

In v.4 Boaz appears on the scene for the first time. Like Naomi, he belongs to the older generation. Ruth's deferential speech (see vv.10, 13; 3:10) recognizes his senior citizen status. He moves about like a patriarch. There is no doubt that Boaz is the lord and master. When he first sees Ruth, he asks to whom she belongs, implying the status quo in a male dominated society. At the same time Boaz displays the virtues of patriarchal magnanimity. He grants privileges to foreign maidens (v.15), going beyond the demands of Lev

19:9; 23:22 with regard to gleaning. He also offers her protection against the young men in the field (v.9). He is also well informed about Ruth, declaring that her devotion to Naomi will not go unrequited (vv.11-12). He is both understanding and consoling; he offers comfort to the oppressed and distressed (v.13).

At the same time the author implies that, although Boaz demonstrates power and influence, he does not determine the flow of events. It is the women who continue to control the course of action. While Boaz will certainly prove his covenant loyalty, it is a loyalty which the women provoke.

The author continues to develop Ruth's leadership role. In v.2 Ruth embarks on a plan of gleaning. Her gleaning is to take place in a field belonging to one in whose eyes she intends to find favor. According to v.10 she has accomplished what she set out to do, viz., she has found favor in Boaz's eyes. Her ingenuity in turn triggers Boaz's recognition of her qualities (v.11). This is indeed in contrast to her apparent anonymity. In v.6 Boaz's employee identifies her as a Moabite who is linked to Naomi. Yet her actions suggest that Ruth is more than an anonymous foreigner. Boaz's blessing in v.12 is like Yahweh's blessing of Abraham in Gen 12. In both cases the recipients of the blessing are foreigners who dare to break with their past in order to serve the God of Israel.

Boaz's blessing challenges the implications of covenant. In his blessing he uses the image of wings. In Deut 32:11 the wings of the eagle offer protection to the young. In Ps 91 [90]:4 Yahweh provides refuge under his wings to the faithful Israelite. In using this image, the author has Boaz test his own sense of covenant loyalty. In 3:9 Ruth will beseech him to spread his wing (RSV: "skirt") over her. Boaz's blessing in chap. 2 remains in the realm of blessing. It can only become a reality when Boaz himself accepts the challenge of protecting Ruth. In the author's theology, to pray or to bless means to have the willingness to reduce the prayer or blessing to reality. Pious prayers without covenantal commitment are unacceptable to the author of Ruth.

RUTH'S RETURN AND CONTINUED GLEANING
2:18-23.

> [18] And she took it up and went into the city; she showed her mother-in-law what she had gleaned, and she also brought out and gave her what food she had left over after being satisfied. [19] And her mother-in-law said to her, "Where did you glean today? And where have you worked? Blessed be the man who took notice of you." So she told her mother-in-law with whom she had worked, and said, "The man's name with whom I worked today is Boaz." [20] And Naomi said to her daughter-in-law, "Blessed be he by the Lord, whose kindness has not forsaken the living or the dead!" Naomi also said to her, "The man is a relative of ours, one of our nearest kin." [21] And Ruth the Moabitess said, "Besides, he said to me, 'You shall keep close by my servants, till they have finished all my harvest.' " [22] And Naomi said to Ruth, her daughter-in-law, "It is well, my daughter, that you go out with his maidens, lest in another field you be molested." [23] So she kept close to the maidens of Boaz, gleaning until the end of the barley and wheat harvests; and she lived with her mother-in-law.

In v.20 Naomi's bitterness begins to dissipate. The mention of Boaz is all the more remarkable since Naomi apparently did not seek him out. In the book itself the two never meet. At this point Naomi reaches out to Ruth, just as Ruth had reached out to her in chap. 1. She now speaks about Boaz as " 'a relative of *ours*, one of *our* nearest kin' " (from the group of family redeemers). Naomi has welcomed her daughter-in-law ever more intimately into the family circle. At the same time her advice matches that given by Boaz, i.e., Ruth is to stay in the company of Boaz's servants (v.22). The woman who clung to her mother-in-law in 1:14 now clings to Boaz's servants (vv.8, 21, 23). The reader begins to suspect that such "clinging" will ultimately resolve the woman's plight.

In this section there is another blessing (see also v.4). In v.20 Naomi acknowledges Boaz's kindness by saying, "'Blessed be he by the Lord, ...'" Like v.4, this is not an idle statement but a profound observation about the interaction of God and humans. Blessing means the release of God's creative power whereby he continues to care for his creatures. However, such release is not limited to the extraordinary moments of life. It looks to the ongoing needs of the community. Blessing is at home in both the field and the sanctuary. Blessing brings these everyday events into the world of God's/humanity's concerns. Ultimately to bless is to impose upon oneself the task of meeting the needs of the members of the covenant community. God thereby continues to provide because the reapers and Naomi provide for Boaz who in turn provides for the women. Blessing is a reality only within the context of community.

It is not-chance-but-providence. In v.3 the author notes that Ruth "happened to come to the part of the field belonging to Boaz ..." In v.4 Boaz happens to come upon the scene at the very time that Ruth is gleaning in the field. By this time the reader realizes that such events are part of God's/humankind's plan to care for the disenfranchised. Similarly the remark in v.23 about the end of the harvests piques the reader's interest. Will it really be an end or will it be another divinely/humanly controlled event which will provoke another step towards resolving the situation of the women?

THE THRESHING FLOOR
3:1-18.

This chapter reveals the same basic structure as chap. 2: the women's planning, execution of the plan, concluding conversation by the women. Although the central section is longer, it is framed by the opening and closing scenes in which the women map out the strategy (compare 2:1-2, 18-22 with 2:3-17). The women are still in control.

The material may be divided as follows: (1) Naomi's plan and Ruth's acceptance (3:1-5); (2) Ruth's execution of the plan (3:6-15); (3) concluding conversation (3:16-18).

NAOMI'S PLAN AND RUTH'S ACCEPTANCE
3:1-5.

3 Then Naomi her mother-in-law said to her, "My daughter, should I not seek a home for you, that it may be well with you? ²Now is not Boaz our kinsman, with whose maidens you were? See, he is winnowing barley tonight at the threshing floor. ³Wash therefore and anoint yourself, and put on your best clothes and go down to the threshing floor; but do not make yourself known to the man until he has finished eating and drinking. ⁴But when he lies down, observe the place where he lies; then, go and uncover his feet and lie down; and he will tell you what to do." ⁵And she replied, "All that you say I will do."

Naomi demonstrates her resourcefulness. In v.1 she refers to her prayer in 1:9. If Ruth is to find a home (and a husband as well), then Naomi must reduce the wishfulness of her prayer to practicality. Although the harvest is over, the winnowing will take place at the threshing floor. Naomi, therefore, resolves to take advantage of the opportunity. The Hebrew text in v.2 may also be translated "gate" rather than "barley." The link between the threshing floor and the gate is supported elsewhere in the Old Testament (see 1 Kgs 22:10). Moreover, this would prepare for the legal transaction at the city gate in chap. 4.

Naomi's ploy involves an erotic element. Ruth's grooming, perfumes, and wardrobe are reminiscent of Esther's beauty treatment (see Esth 2:12-18) and Judith's female warrior apparel (see Jdt 10:3-4). In controlling the course of action, the women thus act in a very feminine manner. The word translated "feet" in v.4 is a euphemism for the genitals (see 1 Sam 24:3, Isa 7:20). The author does not rule out the possibility of sexual intercourse. His ambiguity invites the reader to entertain the possibility. At this point the shrewd mother-in-law assures the equally resourceful daughter-in-law that Boaz will then take over and inform her what to do.

RUTH'S EXECUTION OF THE PLAN
3:6-15.

[6]So she went down to the threshing floor and did just as her mother-in-law had told her. [7]And when Boaz had eaten and drunk, and his heart was merry, he went to lie down at the end of the heap of grain. Then she came softly, and uncovered his feet, and lay down. [8]At midnight the man was startled, and turned over, and behold, a woman lay at his feet! [9]He said, "Who are you?" And she answered, "I am Ruth, your maidservant; spread your skirt over your maidservant, for you are next of kin." [10]And he said, "May you be blessed by the Lord, my daughter; you have made this last kindness greater than

the first, in that you have not gone after young men, whether poor or rich. [11]And now, my daughter, do not fear, I will do for you all that you ask, for all my fellow townsmen know that you are a woman of worth. [12]And now it is true that I am a near kinsman, yet there is a kinsman nearer than I. [13]Remain this night, and in the morning, if he will do the part of the next of kin for you, well; let him do it; but if he is not willing to do the part of the next of kin for you, then, as the Lord lives, I will do the part of the next of kin for you. Lie down until the morning."

[14]So she lay at his feet until the morning, but arose before one could recognize another; and he said, "Let it not be known that the woman came to the threshing floor." [15]And he said, "Bring the mantle you are wearing and hold it out." So she held it, and he measured out six measures of barley, and laid it upon her; then she went into the city.

As compared with the first encounter between Ruth and Boaz, this scene is significantly different. In the first scene the meeting was a matter of "chance" whereas here it is clearly a matter of choice. With regards to the place the public setting of the field gives way to the private atmosphere of the threshing floor. In terms of time the first scene transpired during the day whereas this occurs at night. Finally, concerning action, the first was certainly work while this is clearly play.

In keeping with the sharp distinction between the first and second meetings, the author elaborates an atmosphere of mystery. According to v.7 Boaz lies down at the far end of the heap of grain. In order to avoid detection, Ruth approaches him "softly." When Boaz wakes up around midnight, he is startled and gropes about (RSV: "turned over" — see Judg 16:29), looking to cover himself with his mantle (v.8). At this point he discovers Ruth lying beside him. Finally Ruth leaves the threshing floor before she can be recognized.

Besides the use of "feet" there are other double meanings in the erotic situation. In v.9 Ruth asks Boaz to spread his skirt over her. The Hebrew word "skirt" is the same as "wings" in 2:12. Boaz is thereby challenged to make good his prayer by marrying Ruth. In Ezek 16:8 Yahweh spreads his skirt over the abandoned baby girl (Jerusalem) and the proceeds to marry her. The author employs the verb "to lie down" eight times (vv. 4, 7, 8, 13, 14), thereby heightening the erotic element.

While the verb "to know" has a wide range of meaning including covenantal knowledge (see 2:1; 3:2), simple observation (see vv.4, 11), and realization (v.18), it is also used for carnal knowledge. In v.3 Ruth is not to make herself known until the proper time. In v.14 it is not to become known that a woman came to the threshing floor. While these last two verses do not admit the sexual connotation, they contribute to the highly charged erotic context. (See also the verb "to go" in vv.4, 7 and compare with 4:13.)

Verse 9 involves two legal procedures which are combined only in the Book of Ruth, viz., levirate marriage and redemption (RSV: " 'next of kin' "). According to Deut 25:5-10, if brothers live together and one of them dies childless, the brother of the dead man (in Latin "levir" means brother-in-law) is to marry his sister-in-law and the first son born of the union is to be recognized as the son of the deceased (see Gen 38). Redemption involves one member of the family coming to the aid of another member. It includes: recovering/keeping family property (Lev 25:25; 27:9-33; Jer 32:6-25), obtaining release of a relative from voluntary slavery (Lev 27:47-55), receiving restitution (Num 5:8), and avenging a murder (Num 35:9-28; 2 Sam 14:6-17).

Strictly speaking, Deut 25:5-10 does not apply since it is not a question of a brother but of a distant relative. However, there was never one common legal code to cover the entire country and much was left no doubt to local practice. In any event, the levirate marriage did not look merely to producing an offspring for the dead husband but also to protecting and supporting the widow and keeping property within the family. As in the matter of redemption, the levirate marriage focused on the needs of the legally vulnerable. Though the Book of Ruth alone combines these two legal practices, the fundamental principles are much the same.

In vv.9-11 Ruth's character is more clearly defined. Boaz no longer asks to whom she belongs (2:5) but rather " 'Who are you?' " He also recognizes her as a woman of worth (see 2:1; also Prov 31:10). More importantly, Ruth asserts her own authority. She disobeys her mother-in-law by not allowing Boaz to take the initiative (v.4). By reminding him of the obligations of the levirate and redemption, she provokes a decision. It is not surprising that Boaz acquiesces in v.11: " 'I will do for you all that you ask.' "

Covenant loyalty is implied in Boaz's willingness to heed Ruth's request. At the same time Boaz acknowledges Ruth's twofold covenant loyalty. In v.10 he mentions the loyalty demonstrated in her concern for Naomi. But he also notes that loyalty shown in his own regard. Ruth has not gone after the young men, i.e., she has not accepted any of their marriage proposals (see Gen 24:5, 8, 31, 39). Boaz reaches out to Ruth because Ruth has reached out to Naomi and himself. Ruth *remains* with Boaz (v.13) just as she first chose to *remain* (RSV 1:16: "lodge") with her mother-in-law.

There is a certain amount of apprehension in the nocturnal encounter. Another relative has a prior claim on Ruth. If that relative assumes the obligation, the matter is concluded. The reader wonders if Boaz will somehow outdo his rival. In any case the reader realizes that Boaz will do all in his power to benefit both Ruth and himself (v.13).

CONCLUDING CONVERSATION
3:16-18.

> [16]And when she came to her mother-in-law, she said, "How did you fare, my daughter?" Then she told her all that the man had done for her, [17]saying, "These six measures of barley he gave to me, for he said, 'You must not go back empty-handed to your mother-in-law.' " [18]She replied, "Wait, my daughter, until you learn how the matter turns out, for the man will not rest, but will settle the matter today."

This scene between Naomi and Ruth is a study in the character of both women. Naomi is anxious to know how Ruth fared. But Ruth's answer is evasive: "she told her all that the man had done for her." Actually she should have related all that she had done to Boaz. The six measures of barley are symbolic of Naomi's new fortune. In 1:21 she lamented that Yahweh had brought her back empty. But now (v.17) Boaz insists that Ruth should not return to her mother-in-law empty-handed. In the final verse Naomi advises patience. Although she has never met Boaz, she is convinced that he will settle the affair that day.

Providence is again at work. In v.2 the end of the harvest leads to the winnowing. While Naomi seizes the opportunity, the author implies that the Lord is also matchmaker. In v.7 Boaz is conveniently stretched out at the far end of the heap of grain. This detail adds to the evidence that God is concerned with the needs of the family. Without being called redeemer (but see Isa 41:14; 43:1, 14) the Lord is playing the redeemer's role together with Boaz.

FROM LITIGATION
TO CELEBRATION
4:1-22.

The legal proceedings now get underway. They are concluded with a prayer which is answered in the birth of a
child. A later hand appended a genealogy which expresses
concern for the Davidic line. It is somewhat ironic that the
males determine the fate of the females in the first part of the
chapter. This is certainly the proper procedure. However,
the females, not the males, have been the catalyst for the
final juridical showdown.

The material may be divided as follows: (1) legal proceedings and a final prayer (4:1-12); (2) the child as answer
to the prayer (4:13-17); (3) an appended genealogy (4:18-22).

LEGAL PROCEEDINGS AND A FINAL PRAYER
4:1-12.

4 And Boaz went up to the gate and sat down there; and
behold, the next of kin, of whom Boaz had spoken, came
by. So Boaz said, "Turn aside, friend; sit down here"; and
he turned aside and sat down. ²And he took ten men of
the elders of the city, and said, "Sit down here"; so they
sat down. ³Then he said to the next of kin, "Naomi, who
has come back from the country of Moab, is selling the
parcel of land which belonged to our kinsman Elimelech.

⁴So I thought I would tell you of it, and say, Buy it in the presence of those sitting here, and in the presence of the elders of my people.If you will redeem it, redeem it; but if you will not, tell me, that I may know, for there is no one besides you to redeem it, and I come after you." And he said, "I will redeem it." ⁵Then Boaz said, "The day you buy that field from the hand of Naomi, you are also buying Ruth the Moabitess, the widow of the dead, in order to restore the name of the dead to his inheritance." ⁶Then the next of kin said, "I cannot redeem it for myself, lest I impair my own inheritance. Take my right of redemption yourself, for I cannot redeem it."

⁷Now this was the custom in former times in Israel concerning redeeming and exchanging: to confirm a transaction, the one drew off his sandal and gave it to the other, and this was the manner of attesting in Israel. ⁸So when the next of kin said to Boaz, "Buy it for yourself," he drew off his sandal. ⁹Then Boaz said to the elders and all the people, "You are witnesses this day that I have bought from the hand of Naomi all that belonged to Elimelech and all that belonged to Chilion and to Mahlon. ¹⁰Also Ruth the Moabitess, the widow of Mahlon, I have bought to be my wife, to perpetuate the name of the dead in his inheritance, that the name of the dead may not be cut off from among his brethren and from the gate of his native place; you are witnesses this day." ¹¹Then all the people who were at the gate, and the elders, said, "We are witnesses. May the Lord make the woman, who is coming into your house, like Rachel and Leah, who together built up the house of Israel. May you prosper in Ephrathah and be renowned in Bethlehem; ¹²and may your house be like the house of Perez, whom Tamar bore to Judah, because of the children that the Lord will give you by this young woman."

The author creates the impression that the attentive Boaz left the threshing floor and immediately proceeded to the business at hand. Once again not-chance-but-providence reveals itself in the sudden arrival of the closer relative (see Gen 24:15). However, the author withholds the name of the relative, suggesting perhaps that anonymity is a form of judgment for his unwillingness to accept Ruth. Boaz then gathers ten elders to make the procedure a valid one (v.2). (According to v.4 the ten represent a larger group of elders; according to v.9 other people have also gathered.)

The author piques the reader's interest by not explaining the source of Boaz's information about the property in v.3. Either Naomi has exhibited her now accustomed shrewdness or Boaz has been overly docile in checking the matter out. However, the two never meet in the book. In any event, it is a matter of buying and selling. However, Boaz slyly delays mentioning Ruth until the very end (v.5). Although the unnamed redeemer is willing to buy the property in v.4, he does not relish the added burden of Ruth (v.6). In such a case he would have to support Ruth and Naomi, provide for the new offspring, and in the end see the property revert to the new heir. To be sure, his inheritance would be impaired.

Verses 7-11a relate the transfer of rights from one relative to another. Verse 7 explains a custom or practice which had fallen into desuetude (see 1 Sam 9:9). From this verse, however, it is not clear whether both parties exchanged sandals or only one gave to the other. Ironically, the would-be redeemer is still called a redeemer in v.8 in the very act of renouncing his prior claim. It would seem that his handing over of the sandal symbolized the transfer of the claim to Boaz. At this point Boaz urges the entire gathering to act as legal witnesses. In v.10 he spells out the implications of the transaction but in a decidedly male way. The act is intended to perpetuate Mahlon's name and thus keep his legal rights alive among the local assembly. The witnesses finally acknowledge the legal transfer.

In vv.11b-12 there are three blessings. The first blessing seeks to overcome Ruth's barrenness. Like Rachel and Leah, she is to provide the men with children (see Gen 29-30). The second blessing focuses on Boaz's age. The witnesses pray that he may be fertile (RSV: "prosper" — see Joel 2:22; Job 21:7) and so leave a name, i.e., offspring. The third blessing looks to Boaz's house, i.e., that the levirate marriage of Boaz and Ruth may be as successful as that of

Judah and Tamar, the parents of Perez (see Gen 38).

THE CHILD AS ANSWER TO THE PRAYER
4:13-17.

> ¹³So Boaz took Ruth and she became his wife; and he
> went in to her, and the Lord gave her conception, and she
> bore a son. ¹⁴Then the women said to Naomi, "Blessed be
> the Lord, who has not left you this day without next of
> kin; and may his name be renowned in Israel!
>
> ¹⁵He shall be to you a restorer of life and a nourisher of
> your old age; for your daughter-in-law who loves you,
> who is more to you than seven sons, has borne him."
> ¹⁶Then Naomi took the child and laid him in her bosom,
> and became his nurse. ¹⁷And the women of the neighbor-
> hood gave him a name, saying, "A son has been born to
> Naomi." They named him Obed; he was the father of
> Jesse, the father of David.

The prayers are quickly heard. In the privacy of their
home, as distinct from the public scene of the legal transac-
tions, Boaz and Ruth conceive a child. After ten years of
barren marriage (1:4) Ruth's conception clearly indicates
that God is involved: "the Lord gave her conception." The
curse of chap. 1 gives way to the blessing of chap. 4.

Naomi who was once the object of the women's pity in
1:19 is now the object of their blessing — the Lord has not
deprived her of a redeemer. In 1:21 Naomi lamented that the
Lord caused her to return empty. But now her grandson
causes her life to return (RSV: " 'restorer of life' "). However, the women's blessing reaches its climax in Ruth. In
Naomi's view she is placed on a higher level than the ideal
number of sons (see 1 Sam 1:8). Naomi then assumes her
position as guardian of the child, not wet-nurse (like Mordecai in Esth 2:7). The women conclude on a note of celebration. (It is possible to translate "gave him a name" (v.17) as
"rejoiced over him" [see Deut 32:3].) Their exclamation is
most telling: " 'A son has been born to Naomi.' "

This exclamation is a fitting conclusion to the women's happiness for Naomi. At the same time it is a corrective of the male-oriented legal deliberations in the beginning of the chapter. The purpose, as expressed in v.11, is to perpetuate Mahlon's name. But according to the women the child is born to Naomi, not Mahlon. In their view the child restores life to an old, yet courageous woman rather than a name to her deceased son. After all the planning and work on the part of Naomi and Ruth it is only proper that the child be the expression of such unflagging devotion,

Verse 17b is the conclusion of the story. The mention of David dovetails with the note about the time of the Judges in 1:1. It is hard to imagine that the author fabricated the note about David's Moabite ancestry. The conclusion, however, does not rule out his creating a story against the back-ground of such ancestry. If the two women had not cared for each other and if Boaz had not reacted to their loyalty, then the great King David would never have been. Covenant loyalty has implications not only for a family's future but also for a nation's future.

AN APPENDED GENEALOGY
4:18-22.

> [18]Now these are the descendants of Perez: Perez was the father of Hezron, [19]Hezron of Ram, Ram of Amminadab, [20]Amminadab of Nahshon, Nahshon of Salmon, [21]Salmon of Boaz, Boaz of Obed, [22]Obed of Jesse, and Jesse of David.

It is generally agreed that this appendix is the work of a later hand. Among other things the story comes to a natural conclusion in v.17b, so that the genealogy necessarily appears anti-climactic. The genealogy itself is similar to the one found in 1 Chr 2:5, 9-15. It is likely that both the later hand in Ruth and the Chronicler borrowed from a common source. Although anti-climactic, the genealogy expresses the human concern for roots. The later hand probably felt the need to anchor David more firmly in the history of his people.

FOR FURTHER READING

GENERAL WORKS

E. Bickerman. *Four Strange Books of the Bible*. New York: Schocken, 1967. This offers a literary appreciation of Esther and Jonah (as well as Qoheleth and Daniel).

J.C. Dancy. *The Shorter Books of the Apocrypha*. The Cambridge Bible Commentary on the New English Bible. Cambridge and New York: Cambridge University Press, 1972. This is a very readable commentary on Judith, Tobit, and the deuterocanonical sections of Esther. The introductions provide useful material for assessing both the theological and literary dimensions of these books.

THE BOOK OF ESTHER

S.B. Berg. *The Book of Esther: Motifs, Themes and Structure*. Society of Biblical Literature Dissertation Series. Missoula: Scholars Press, 1979. As the title indicates, this is a study which focuses on the literary dimensions of Esther. It is excellent for understanding the author's way of telling the story.

C.A. Moore. *Esther*. Anchor Bible. Garden City: Doubleday, 1971. This is a solid commentary with an invaluable introduction. The notes are extremely useful.

C.A. Moore. *Daniel, Esther and Jeremiah: The Additions*. Anchor Bible. Garden City: Doubleday, 1977. This treats the deuterocanonical sections of Esther. Once again both the introduction and notes are very helpful.

THE BOOK OF JUDITH

L. Alonso Schökel et al. *Narrative Structures in the Book of Judith*. Protocol Series of the Colloquies of the Center for Hermeneutical Studies in Hellenistic and Modern Culture. Berkeley: Graduate Theological Union, 1975. This slender volume consists of Alonso Schökel's paper and the colloquy between him and seven respondents. It is an excellent study for appreciating Judith as a piece of literature. It is much more significant for understanding Judith than its slender seventy-two pages would indicate.

T. Craven. "Artistry and Faith in the Book of Judith," *Semeia* 8 (1977) 75-101. This article focuses on the chiastic structure of the book and its stylistic features. Chaps. 1-7 are thereby brought into sharper and closer contact with chaps. 8-16. Its insights are particularly useful for understanding the first seven chapters.

M.S. Enslin and S. Zeitlin. *The Book of Judith*. Jewish Apocryphal Literature. Leiden: Brill, 1972. Both the introduction and the commentary offer a wealth of information on philological, text-critical, and historical problems. The volume should be supplemented with the rhetorical criticism approach of Alonso Schökel and Craven.

THE BOOK OF TOBIT

A.A. DiLella. "The Deuteronomic Background of the Farewell Discourse in Tob 14:3-11," *Catholic Biblical Quarterly* 41 (1979) 380-389. This is an invaluable study of the influence of Deuteronomy in the Book of Tobit.

Although the article deals specifically with Tob 14:3-11, it also establishes the Deuteronomic influence elsewhere in the book.

F. Zimmerman. *The Book of Tobit*. Jewish Apocryphal Literature. New York: Harper, 1958. This commentary has an extensive introduction which covers a variety of interests. It is technical but readable.

THE BOOK OF JONAH

T. E. Fretheim. *The Message of Jonah. A Theological Commentary*. Minneapolis: Augsburg, 1977. This is an extremely readable yet penetrating study of the theology of Jonah. It is especially rewarding in its analysis of irony, structure, and unity.

T. E. Fretheim. "Jonah and Theodicy," *Zeitschrift für die alttestamentliche Wissenschaft* 90 (1978) 227-237. This is a challenging article which deals with the purpose of Jonah. The author offers the insight that the book is about God's radical ability to be a giver of gifts in the absence of any claims. The book celebrates divine freedom.

H.W. Wolff. *Jonah: Church in Revolt*. St. Louis: Clayton, 1979. This is a provocative commentary on Jonah which also reduces its message to modern pastoral practice. It is also very useful for the structure of the book.

THE BOOK OF RUTH

E.F. Campbell, Jr. *Ruth*. Anchor Bible. Garden City: Doubleday, 1975. The commentary offers all the advantages of the Anchor Bible series. Its analysis of Ruth as a Hebrew short story is especially useful. Though quite detailed at times, it is still very readable.

R.M. Hals. *The Theology of the Book of Ruth.* Facet Books. Philadelphia: Fortress, 1969. This study sees Ruth as a product of the period of Solomonic enlightenment. It is a helpful work for appreciating the role of humans in making the hidden God of Israel present to their world.

P. Trible. "Two Women in a Man's World: A Reading of the Book of Ruth," *Soundings* 59 (1976) 251-279. See expanded version in: *God and the Rhetoric of Sexuality.* Overtures to Biblical Theology. Philadelphia: Fortress, 1978. Pp. 166-199. The author approaches Ruth from the vantage point of rhetorical criticism. Ruth is thus seen as a human comedy. A great advantage of this study is an appreciation of Ruth and Naomi from a woman's point of view. Basically it explores human liberation.